3333318109923

D0720662

WITHDRAWN. FOR FREE USE IN CITY
CULTURAL AND WELFARE INSTITUTIONS
MAY BE SOLD FOR THE BENEFIT OF
THE NEW YORK PUBLIC LIBRARY ONLY.

THE VENERABLE ADRIENNE HOWLEY was ordained in 1982 by His Holiness the Dalai Lama. In 1993 she took the highest ordination vows possible from a Vietnamese Buddhist master, thus becoming one of the very few Western women in the world to have done so. A former nurse and the mother of two sons, she has sailed around the world, survived a life-threatening cancer, and is the author of a biography of the noted Australian poet, Dorothea Mackellar. Now in her early seventies, she lives in a small rural town north of Sydney, Australia, where she devotes her time to Buddhist practice and teaching, as well as doing volunteer work in a local hospice.

THE NAKED BUDDHA

THE NAKED BUDDHA

A Practical Guide to the
Buddha's Life and Teachings

VENERABLE ADRIENNE HOWLEY

MARLOWE & COMPANY
NEW YORK

THE NAKED BUDDHA: *A Practical Guide to the Buddha's Life and Teachings*
Copyright © 1999, 2002, 2003 by Venerable Adrienne Howley

Published by
Marlowe & Company
An Imprint of Avalon Publishing Group Incorporated
245 West 17th Street • 11th Floor
New York, NY 10011-5300

This is a conflated edition of *The Naked Buddha* and
The Naked Buddha Speaks, originally published by Bantam Books,
Australia, in 1999 and 2002 respectively.
This edition published by arrangement with Random House Australia.

All rights reserved. No part of this book may be reproduced in whole or in
part without written permission from the publisher, except by reviewers
who may quote brief excerpts in connection with a review in a newspaper,
magazine, or electronic publication; nor may any part of this book be
reproduced, stored in a retrieval system, or transmitted in any form or by
any means electronic, mechanical, photocopying, recording, or other,
without written permission from the publisher.

Library of Congress Cataloging-in-Publication Data

Howley, Adrienne, 1926–
    The naked Buddha : a beginner's guide to the Buddha's life
and teachings / Venerable Adrienne Howley.
        p. cm.
    Includes bibliographical references.
    ISBN 1-56924-432-4 (pbk)
    1. Gautama Buddha—Teachings.   2. Buddhism—Doctrines.
    3. Buddhists—India—Biography.   I. Title.

BQ915.H6 2004
294.3—dc22

                                                        2003066644

ISBN 1-56924-432-4

9   8   7   6   5   4   3   2   1

DESIGNED BY PAULINE NEUWIRTH, NEUWIRTH & ASSOCIATES, INC.

Printed in the United States of America

IN GRATITUDE FOR THE DHARMA
THAT TURNS BITTERNESS INTO NECTAR
AND HATRED INTO LOVE

[CONTENTS]

[INTRODUCTION]

$\mathcal{T}$HE TITLE OF this book—*The Naked Buddha*—illustrates my attempt to strip away stereotypical views of Buddhism, respectfully laying to one side the cultural trappings under which the Buddha's original ideas have become almost hidden from view, so that you, the reader, may meet these teachings directly.

The Buddha's teachings offer layers of meaning, depending how far the student wants to go. What I write about here is basic, down-to-earth, non-mystical Buddhism. Those who want a deeper understanding will find it. This is simply an effort to show the non-practitioner what lies behind the beliefs of five hundred million people around the world.

Like all religions, Buddhism has devotional adherents among its followers. As I am not the devotional type, I seek to strip the Buddha of added layers and coverings and get down to what he really thought and taught, as closely as I can. My way is not better than that of the devotee, only different. This is a matter of individual psychological makeup. We seek what we need most.

Buddhism has spread into many cultures over more than twenty-five hundred years. In the process, it has absorbed many of the beliefs of these cultures. As a result, there is a great diversity of adornment in Buddhist churches and great differences in rituals and the focus of ceremonies. These can be unintelligible without study of the political, social, religious and philosophical background of the people who are practicing their version of Buddhism.

At first contact, these cultural trappings look confusing, and the profound philosophy underneath is veiled from our gaze. Who was the founder of all this? Do the statues of the Buddha represent a god? Do they represent a savior, or a hero from the past? A mythological being? Are they abstract representations of an ideal? Of a human person?

Amid all the cultural and religious pageantry, ritual and ceremony, the basic Buddhist teachings have remained unchanged since the time of the Buddha. In this book, I hope you will find short, clear accounts of the human being who became the Buddha, as well as the main points of what he taught and how best to go about approaching an understanding of his teachings.

My aim in this book is to inspire religious, racial and cultural tolerance through *understanding.* I hope to achieve this through explanations based on my own studies and experiences. My reason for attempting this is to help counter the type of religious strife and persecution seen in so many parts of our world today. There is nothing pertaining to the Buddhist religion that should cause anxiety in the minds or emotions of others. There is no custom of converting people to Buddhism. Quite the contrary, no Buddhist will *tell* you anything unless you ask. The present writer would not have put pen to paper without being asked to do so. But once the questions are asked, there is a wealth of information to be had—and the subject of Buddhism is interesting and topical.

What I find most interesting about Buddhism is that the Buddha taught for forty years and then invited his followers not to believe a word he had told them until they had investigated it for themselves. He did not demand unquestioned obedience and devotion, unlike many who set themselves up as teachers of Buddhism today. He taught mental alertness, constant investigation and clear-sightedness, among other things.

I am a fully ordained Buddhist nun. I was first ordained into the Tibetan tradition by Tenzin Gyatso, His Holiness the fourteenth Dalai Lama and six high lamas, and later into the Vietnamese tradition by Master Thich Huyen Vi and ten male and female elders. The second ordination was necessary because I wished to receive the highest ordination, and the Theravadin and Tibetan traditions don't hold this lineage for women. But if you asked me to what tradition I now belong, I prefer to be known as what I call "a Buddha Buddhist."

I am one of a very loose group known as wandering monks and nuns who do not often live in organized monasteries and who teach whenever requested to do so. When you give up the support of monastic life, as I have done, you do the best you can according to your means. I do voluntary work in the community. I don't shave my head these days, having found that my hair seems to give me a better rapport with my fellow citizens and clients in the West.

I am not religious in the sense of relying on rites and rituals. I avoid organized religion with its ready-made tenets and -isms because for me things of the "spirit" are personal and a matter of continual learning. I don't tell you this in order to sound like a Buddhist expert. I can speak only of what I have learned from my own studies and investigations, and from the teachings I received from those more learned than myself.

Buddhism is about *enlightenment*, and enlightenment means fully understanding. Gautama Buddha taught from experience. He did not receive divine directions or messages from gods. He was a human being who married and had children. There was nothing mysterious about his life. He was extremely intelligent and earnest in his search for a way for sentient beings to understand and overcome suffering. He left his comfortable life to study for seven years with the greatest teachers of his place and time, even putting his life at risk in order to learn.

Eventually, he began to investigate for himself, relying only on his own efforts. This is when his *enlightenment,* or full understanding, began to unfold.

Having found the cause of suffering and the way out of it by his own efforts, the Buddha then wondered if people would really want to know. Would they bother to listen? Then compassion for all sentient beings caused him to begin teaching what he had learned. For the next forty-five years, the Buddha taught and gave advice to people from all walks of life—from royalty, to businessmen, to the caste that later was called the "untouchables." He taught according to the needs and capabilities of his listeners.

The Buddha was no dogmatist. His constant injunction was that his listeners not believe what he said simply out of respect for him, but that they investigate matters for themselves. This is what a real Buddhist tries to do. What we learn is eventually a personal experience for each of us.

My initial contact with Buddhism happened more than thirty years ago when my oldest son handed me a book called *The Teachings of the Compassionate Buddha*. The contents grabbed my attention, but there were no qualified teachers in my area at that time so I just read what came my way. I was far too busy making a mess of my life to do more than that.

Whenever life got to be a bit much, I would joke that one day I would either live on top of Mount Everest or become a Buddhist nun. The joke became a self-fulfilling prophecy.

Although I am a Buddhist nun, I may disappoint those seeking mystery and magic from "beyond." The Buddha didn't deal in such ideas. I have based my own thinking on the earliest material about him that I have been able to discover, the original investigations having been done by qualified scholars.

Buddhism is many layered. It has almost as many layers as there are believers and certainly as many layers as there are *cultural* beliefs onto which the basic teachings have been grafted. Much of what is written in this book would probably not be recognized by many who consider themselves Buddhists.

I would like to emphasize, again, that in this book I am speaking on the mundane level of basic Buddhist teachings. To speak on any other level would require a different work. This book is written for the ordinary person who is trying to live as happily and comfortably as possible in the world in which we have to function. It is also written for those who are open-minded and mentally flexible enough to consider a different point of view, whether merely out of curiosity or in the hope of finding a way out of unnecessary suffering. I believe I have written just clearly enough to stimulate further investigation—which is what Buddhism is all about.

I don't profess to be a teacher but as anyone who knows me will agree, I love to talk about Buddhism. That is what I do in this book. To those who want to listen, I wish you a wonderful journey, wherever it may lead.

ADRIENNE HOWLEY LORN, 2003

THE NAKED BUDDHA

ONE

THE HISTORICAL BUDDHA

*W*HO WAS THE BUDDHA?

*W*HO WAS THIS person whom so many people refer to as *the Buddha?* What did he do or say that had such a momentous effect on his own people while he lived, and was heard in most parts of the known world of his time? When and where did this person live? Why did he find it necessary to teach something new in a land that already had a strong functioning religious structure in place—Brahminism. Why did *his* teachings take hold so firmly when so many others were philosophizing deeply about life?

Historical records, modern knowledge of ancient customs and archaeology can tell us enough to construct a simple, straightforward picture of the life of the Buddha. Stories from folklore and stories inspired by devotion have added a great deal of improbable decoration to the picture—a price paid by anyone who comes to public notice.

There are many stories of his early life, mostly legend and folklore with religious overtones—a pure birth from Queen Maya's side; words spoken by the newly born infant and steps taken toward the compass points; the story of him never becoming aware of sickness, poverty and death until adulthood; his prophetic horoscope; and his leaving behind a newborn son and sneaking off into the night, never to return to his home as a son, husband or father.

The given name of the Buddha was Siddhartha, and his family name was Gautama. He was the heir to his father, Suddhodana, elected king of the Sakyas, a wealthy clan whose state lay partly in what is now the western area of Nepal. Siddhartha was born in about 543 B.C., at the time of the full moon, during our month of May, in a place called the Lumbini Gardens. His mother was Queen Maya, Suddhodana's first wife. From widespread reading and study of the political, religious and social conditions in India in the sixth century B.C., as well as from the interpretation of some archaeological finds, it is likely that the son of King Suddhodana and Queen Maya may have been born by Caesarean section and needed assistance to breathe. This is because the oldest texts say that the infant was washed in cold and warm water—in that order. I was a midwife and trained nurse, and I can see the baby being splashed with cold water from the tank to stimulate respiration (still a common practice) and only then being bathed with warm water as newborn infants are.

The water the infant was washed in came from the tank in the Lumbini Gardens where Maya, on her way back to her family home for the birth (as custom demanded) went into labor. As some of you may have seen, the tanks in the Lumbini Gardens are stone-lined pools and hardly sterile. The Queen was also washed with the tank water and died seven days later, either from loss of blood or postpartum infection. Maya's sister, who had been Suddhodana's second wife, became the baby's foster mother. She was already the mother of a son, Davida, a jealous half-brother of Siddhartha. Davida later tried unsuccessfully to kill his rival sibling, and he gathered a following of his own, attempting to discredit Siddhartha and his teachings.

The new baby's horoscope was cast, and it was foretold that he would become a famous warrior ruler—as befitted his caste— or a great spiritual teacher. Although the child Siddhartha was showered with all the pleasures his father and the Sakyas could bestow on him, he grew up to be rather serious-minded. He was given the best available secular and religious education, being groomed as the future political and military leader of his clan.

In India, in the sixth century B.C., people were divided into castes based on skin color due to repeated invasions by light-skinned, blue-eyed people (the Aryans) from the northwest. These invaders forced the indigenous population further and further southward and they, in turn, displaced the earlier inhabitants. Breeding between invaders and the people who were conquered was responsible for different skin tones. As elsewhere in the world, this tended to categorize people socially. Later, caste became a matter of birth.

In order of status the caste system was as follows:

Brahmins: Hereditary priests of the main Indian religion, believing Brahma to be their creator. The Brahmin priests were the only possible mediators between gods and goddesses and human beings. Only Brahmins could make sacrifices and read the resulting omens. No one could rise to be a Brahmin. You had to be born to that status. The Brahmins grew rich on offerings from the people who paid the priests to perform ceremonies to placate the gods, to conduct rituals for betrothals, marriages and deaths, and to read the future from the stars.

Ksatriya: The military and ruling class whose duties were to guard the people and the land. Many considered the Ksatriya even more important than the Brahmins. All leaders, chieftains and kings of various areas, military captains and political administrators belonged to this group—as did the Buddha's clan.

Vaisya: Merchants and skilled workers. This group was made up of traders, businesspeople and those whose caravans carried all the local news and gossip within their own country and into the countries of trading partners. They were agriculturalists, trades people, workers in metal, stone and fabrics, artists and so on.

Sudra: Mostly unskilled workers. These were small, dark-skinned people, probably the original inhabitants of India. They were taken over by Aryan and other invaders over the centuries. Later, they came to be called "the untouchables" and were given the most unpleasant societal tasks to perform, but this was not yet the case in the sixth century B.C.

Slaves: Usually foreigners and prisoners of war. Their circumstances depended on their owners. They might be treated as anything, from mere property to a friend.

In this system, one caste did not marry into another except on rare occasions. This was as much due to preference as to custom. And Brahmins married only Brahmins, considering all others to be of lower caste.

Although the priests held enormous influence over the minds of the people, there are always some people who want to delve more deeply into the why's and how's of life than what is explained by the existing religion. In the Buddha's time, these became wandering ascetics who lived in the forests for long periods. These *forest dwellers* were fed by devoted followers or lived on herbs and fruits. Only during the monsoon period did they need more shelter than the shade of a tree.

Family life in India was of great importance in the sixth century B.C. It became acceptable for men or women to become forest dwellers or wandering seekers-after-wisdom only after family
duties had been attended to. First heirs had to be produced, wives
and parents had to be provided for, if necessary, and the consent
of families had to be sought and received. Naturally, many wanderers simply absconded from their responsibilities.

Marriage took place quite early in life, as is still the custom
in India today. At sixteen years old, or even earlier, for all physical intents and purposes a boy was considered ready for marriage. Siddhartha Gautama, a member of the warrior and ruling
class, was no exception. He was married during his teens, some-
time between the ages of sixteen and eighteen, to his cousin, the
daughter of a neighboring ruler. Her name was Yasodhara, and
she brought a rich dowry to the marriage as well as many hand-
maidens and friends—again, this was the custom.

Siddhartha led the life of any healthy young man of wealth in
a loving, indulgent family. It is possible that daughters were born
to Yasodhara and even sons to his concubines, but unless they
personally achieved fame daughters were rarely listed in the history of that time. The first son of the first wife became the heir.
Most stories agree that Siddhartha was nearly twenty-nine when
Yasodhara bore a son, although this may have happened at an
earlier date. The child was named Rahula; and later, he became
one of his father's disciples and a monk.

How and Why Did the Buddha Become a Teacher?

TRADITIONAL STORIES STATE that during the Buddha's childhood he was sheltered from the facts of old age, sickness and death. This was his father's scheme for keeping his son safe from part of the prophecy given at his birth—that he could become a great spiritual teacher. Naturally, the father hoped his first-born would follow in his own footsteps and become a great warrior leader instead.

Everything that Siddhartha could desire was given to him. He was educated and trained for war and leadership. However, eventually the vigilance of his attendants fell short of the King's instructions. While on a state visit outside the royal precincts, Siddhartha became aware of human suffering—poverty, illness, anger, greed and death. He also encountered a monk who explained the possibility of a contemplative life to him. The seed was born in his mind to try to discover the cause of suffering and, if possible, to overcome it. By the time he was twenty-nine, he had made up his mind to begin his search.

It helps to know something of the customs of Indian society at the time, to understand Siddhartha's actions at this point. In Siddhartha's caste, once an heir had been produced and survived childhood, the parents (usually the father) were free to pursue their search for understanding. One duty remained—dependents had to be provided for, and these dependents had to be willing to let the seeker go. Often husbands and wives set off together on their quest.

At the age of twenty-nine, saturated with the good life, Siddhartha set out on his own search. He became a forest dweller, a seeker after the reasons for human suffering and a way out of such suffering.

Some Western interpretations of this part of Siddhartha Gautama's story tell a harrowing tale of his abandoning his loving young wife and newborn baby in the dead of night to go on his quest for understanding and truth. Had this been true, the Buddha would never have commanded the love and respect he held not only from his clan and his wife but from others as well. Instead, Siddhartha Gautama did what was the norm for his place, caste and time. He trained as a warrior and future leader of his tribe. He was well educated by the best available tutors in religion, politics and economics. He married suitably and produced a legal heir, Rahula. Having done this, he was free to become a homeless one, a wandering seeker after wisdom. By then he was no discontented youth. He was a deep thinker and twenty-nine years of age. He left his home—again as was often the custom—and spent the next seven years learning from the wisest and most well known religious and philosophical teachers of India.

He tried out for himself their methods of gaining insight into the fundamental principles of existence and the cause of human suffering. Some taught indulgence in excessive eating, drinking and sexual practices in order to learn disgust for the desires of the body. Some ate only one herb or fruit. Some practiced self- or other-inflicted torture. Some practiced all types of yogic exercises and deep trance. Some participated in deep philosophical discussions. From none of these practices did Siddhartha find the answers he sought.

The final practice he underwent at this time was long and drastic fasting. This caused him to become so emaciated and weak that as he entered a stream one morning to bathe, he came close to drowning. After this he broke his fast and accepted some food, for which his fellow wanderers—five ascetics—scorned him. Then he reviewed his experiences of the past seven years and realized that none of them had led to the wisdom he sought.

When his health recovered, he made a vow to sit beneath the pipal tree (a type of ficus) and meditate until either he found the wisdom he sought or he died. This tree, later known as the *bodhi* tree—referring to the notion of "awake" in Sanskrit—was at Bodh Gaya in India. A slip was taken from the original tree; and since then, before each generation of this bodhi tree dies, a slip of the tree is planted on the same spot. Next to Kusinara, where the Buddha died, Bodh Gaya has become the most revered place for Buddhist pilgrims.

Siddhartha sat on a heap of grass, in what we call the *lotus position,* his palms up on his lap, right on left, and began his momentous quest. For several days he made little headway, wrestling with the temptation to give up. Since he was fasting, he suffered hallucinations. Finally, mentally exhausted, he relinquished his intellectual process, quieted his mind and—just as we often find the answer to a worrisome problem when we give up battling with it—Siddhartha made a breakthrough. What he sought suddenly became clear to him. This was not a miracle but the result of his own efforts. Now he had become the Buddha, the *Enlightened One,* "the awakened one" (in Sanskrit *buddha* means "awake").

There are great differences between the Buddha and leaders of other religions. He was not and never professed to be the offspring of any god. He did not receive messages and instructions from mysterious sources. He was a normal human being born of human parents who fulfilled all the functions of a human being—nothing supernatural, unless you consider his great courage, determination, intellectual capacity and universal compassion as being above the norm. He never claimed his was the only way but only invited those who wished to do so to try it. Buddhism is not a proselytizing religion. The Buddha's teachings are called "the Dharma"—*dharma* means "law" in Sanskrit. They are taught only to individuals or groups who ask for it. In Buddhism, the teacher does not seek the student.

After becoming enlightened, the Buddha wasn't sure if what he had realized would be understood by others. After a lengthy consideration, he realized that what he had learned could be of immense help to sentient (conscious) beings. He decided to share what he had learned out of compassion for the suffering caused by ignorance. His first sermon was to the five ascetics who mocked him for breaking his long fast. He explained to them his enlightenment—his coming to understand suffering, the cause of suffering, and the way out of suffering. On the basis of their own long and sincere search, these five ascetics immediately understood. They knew that this was indeed a Buddha, an Enlightened One, and they became his first disciples.

Siddhartha Gautama, now the Buddha, went on from there to teach constantly until he died at over eighty years of age. Some people followed him for most of their lives yet never really understood his words. Others, on hearing the teaching once from the Buddha or from an enlightened disciple, were instantly able to comprehend the meaning and became enlightened.

The Buddha accepted everyone who came to hear him—from kings, Brahmins and wandering ascetics to householders and the lowest caste. And he accepted women also.

Although the Buddha told his first followers to travel—they went as far as Libya—they did not do what we understand as missionary work. They spoke only to those who wanted to listen or those who were seeking wisdom. As mentioned, this remains the Buddhist practice—no knocking on doors, no propaganda of any kind. The seeker finds the teacher, not the other way around.

In Buddhism it's important to note that the teaching is the important thing—not the teacher. The Buddha's final injunction was to believe nothing he said but to investigate—investigate for oneself. We can all do that.

*W*HAT DID HE LOOK LIKE?

ANCIENT RECORDS TELL us that the Buddha had blue eyes. This is not unlikely, because blue eyes are not uncommon in the area where he was born. Another record, said to be his own reply to a question put to him by a Brahmin, says that he was six feet tall. In other records, he is said to have had a serene, compassionate expression, and it is said that he often smiled. There are even some records of him rebuking certain disciples, so he was not a soft or insipid teacher.

In addition to these quite believable descriptions of the Buddha, there are others which are harder to believe—such as the story of his having hair in which every curl turned in one direction, certain descriptions of his genitalia, accounts of webbing between his fingers and toes, and imprints of a "wheel of life" on the soles of his feet. These are pre-Buddhist beliefs, said to be the marks of a superior man, which were brought in by Brahmin followers in later times.

One particular mark of the superior man is more easily understood—elongated earlobes. This is another pre-Buddhist belief, also found in other places in the world. It comes from the fact that in certain cultures the rich wore heavy earrings. The richer (and therefore heavier) the ornaments, the more they stretched the wearer's earlobes. It is probable the Buddha in his domestic life had worn ornate earrings, but records indicate he did not do so after setting out on his quest for enlightenment.

Later, he discouraged this practice in his disciples once they became what we today call monks and nuns.

WHO WERE HIS FOLLOWERS?

BUDDHISM IS NOT only for those capable of ascetic practices, hermits, scholars, philosophers, monks and nuns. Buddhism is not beyond the power of ordinary people to understand and practice. The teachings are *for* ordinary people. The teachings may even help ordinary people to become *extraordinary* people. Monasteries were only an outcome of Buddhism, not the intended outcome of the Buddha's wish to share his understanding. The Buddha taught ordinary laypeople—some of whom later became monks and nuns because that was their need—but his teaching was for all. It was not expected that anyone would change his or her way of life unless it was causing, or was capable of causing, harm to others— such as murdering, thieving or working in armaments or poisons.

The caste system was taken very seriously by members of the Brahmin caste. Their religious texts, the *Vedas,* state that if the lowest caste spoke about the Vedas their tongues would be split. If they listened, their ears would be filled with molten lead. However, the Buddha made no distinctions based on caste lines or on other types of discrimination. He spoke to anyone or any group coming to hear what he had to say.

We should note that monks and nuns are not necessarily the *best* Buddhists. The *best* Buddhists—monks, nuns or laypeople—are those who strive to understand correctly what *really is*. The best are those who strive to analyze their own concepts, their own view of existence and the reasons why they react as they do. They are the ones who strive to be constantly aware of what is happening around and within themselves, the ones for whom doing no harm has effortlessly become their way of living. Buddhists are not expected to emulate a god or a supernatural being. The goal of enlightenment is achievable by any earnest person in this very lifetime.

After the Buddha had instructed his first disciples and was satisfied they understood what he had told them, he sent them out to repeat the teaching. By word of mouth, the Buddha then became a much-sought-after teacher. Kings sought him out for personal and practical as well as philosophical advice. Due to his previous social standing, he was welcome in palaces and among the well educated, but his more general teachings usually took place in the open so that an unrestricted audience could gather.

When asked for advice by kings and rulers, Buddha told them to rule with justice and see to the well-being of their subjects. He pointed out that poverty was a cause of robbery, and therefore, workers should be paid just wages. Attention should be paid to seeing that storehouses were kept stocked against times of need such as drought, floods and other natural disasters. He gave advice about the likely outcome of armed conflict with neighboring states.

Business people also sought the Buddha's advice. To these, he said to treat workers and servants with kindness and fairness in all matters. His advice to workers and servants was to work honestly and diligently. He also advised business people to divide their income into four and use one part for business purposes, one part for their own needs and the maintenance of their family, one part for charitable concerns and the fourth part for future needs.

There was never anything in his teaching that inflamed his listeners or led to wild behavior, so rulers and wealthy people offered the Buddha parks and groves in their own domains for use as meeting places and retreat centers. Retreats were held during the rainy season when foot travel was almost impossible and often dangerous. To this day, Buddhist monks and nuns, as well as many laypeople, hold a retreat between May and August, full-time if possible. Of course, for those in monasteries this is easy, but for self-supporting Western Buddhists, participating in a full-time retreat can be difficult.

With the passing of years, the number of Buddha's followers increased rapidly. Most were people who flocked to hear him whenever he was in their area, but there were others who wanted more instruction than they could get from an occasional talk. There were also those who wished to devote their lives to learning all they could from their teacher. Beginning with the first five ascetics, they became the first members of the *Sangha* (*sangha* is Sanskrit for "community," or community of monks and nuns).

Not only men wished to hear the Buddha's words. Queens and courtesans, wealthy women, housewives and young unwed girls all came to hear this new wisdom. They made offerings of food and land and invited their teacher and his chief disciples into their homes. The Buddha made no distinction between men and women. He spoke in exactly the same way to all.

$\mathcal{D}$ID THE BUDDHA TEACH BELIEF AND FAITH?

BUDDHISM DOES NOT teach blind faith or belief. What is required is seeing existence as clearly as we can and being as free of our concepts and misperceptions as possible. The Buddha often used parables to help his listeners understand him, and the parable of the raft is still a favorite one. Buddha likened his teachings to a raft constructed for the safe crossing of troubled waters. Once across the stream, it is pointless to hoist the raft onto one's back and continue clinging to it on the safe shore. Much better to leave it for those who might be able to use it. The one who has already crossed the stream (who has fully understood the Dharma) no longer needs the raft because it has fulfilled its purpose.

$\mathcal{Q}$UESTIONING THE BUDDHA

DURING HIS TEACHING life, which spanned more than forty-five years, the Buddha was perpetually questioned by those seeking knowledge and those trying to refute his philosophy. He consistently refused to contend with his questioners on any subject of a metaphysical nature. He neither agreed nor disagreed, telling such questioners that imaginative speculation on certain subjects was useless.

One such questioner was his own disciple, Malunkyaputta. This student realized that many of the problems he had repeatedly put to his teacher had been put aside without explanation, so he decided at last to demand clarification. Malunkyaputta presented ten problems for clarification to the Buddha:

1. Is the universe eternal? Or . . .
2. Is it not eternal?
3. Is the universe finite? Or . . .
4. Is it infinite?
5. Is the soul (spirit) the same as the body? Or . . .
6. Is the soul one thing and the body another?
7. Does the *Tathagata* (another term used for a fully enlightened one) exist after death? Or . . .
8. Does he not exist after death?
9. Does he both (simultaneously) not exist or exist after death? Or . . .
10. Does he both (simultaneously) not exist and not not exist?

Malunkyaputta obviously spent much time thinking!

In response, the Buddha asked this disciple if he had ever said to him, "Come, lead the holy life under me, and I will explain these questions to you." He also asked if Malunkyaputta had ever said to him, "Sir, I will lead the holy life under the Blessed One, and he will explain these questions to me." Buddha also said that if someone refused to lead the holy life under him until these questions were explained, that person would die with the questions unanswered. Then he told Malunkyaputta the following parable:

Suppose a man is wounded by a poison arrow and is brought to the doctor. Now suppose the man refuses to be treated until he knows who shot him, whether he is a member of this or that class, what his name and family might be, whether he is short or tall or of medium height, whether his complexion is black, brown or golden, and which town or village he comes from. Suppose the sick man says he will not be treated until he knows the kind of bow with which he was shot, the kind of bowstring used, the type of arrow, what sort of feather was on the arrow, and what sort of material the point of the arrow was made of.

The Buddha explained that the man would die before he knew the answers to those questions. He explained to Malunkyaputta that whatever *opinion* one might have about the questions asked, there still remained the very real problems of birth, old age, decay, death, sorrow, pain, grief and distress—the cessation of which Buddha *had* explained. To explain *these* matters, he said, was useful and helpful in avoiding unskillful behavior and gaining nonattachment, tranquility and full realization.

This seemed to set Malunkyaputta on a new train of thought, because elsewhere he is reported to have approached the Buddha later on for further instruction and to have become enlightened.

$\mathcal{M}$EAT OR VEGETABLES?

IT IS COMMONLY thought that to be a Buddhist means to be a strict vegetarian. Not so. The reason behind vegetarianism in Buddhist religious practice is the general rule of conduct (one of FIVE PRECEPTS) not to kill. The original idea behind this precept is that all life is sacred, and therefore, to kill animals and birds for religious sacrifice, as was done at the time, is cruel and unnecessary. It demonstrates no compassion for the slaughtered sacrificial animals.

It should be noted that precepts are not commandments. These general rules of conduct are not Buddhist "thou shall not's." If there is anything close to a commandment, it is this— THINK. Think about what you are doing, why you are doing it and what could be some of the most likely outcomes. In this respect, Buddhists attempt to act skillfully rather than unskillfully and to avoid extremes of behavior. They attempt to follow what Buddhists call *the middle way.*

Naturally, you can do only the best you can. Vegetarianism is easy in countries where fruits and vegetables are easily grown. Where extensive raising of vegetables for food is not part of the culture, such as in Tibet and Mongolia, meat is a necessary part of the diet. In China and Japan, fish and soybean products provide necessary protein. Fowl, eggs and fish do this in other cultures.

Originally, the Buddha's monks and nuns took their begging bowls into the town or village in the morning, and village people each gave a little of what they could. This was then taken back to the group and shared as the one meal of the day, eaten just before noon.

The earliest Buddhist teaching on this subject—said to be Buddha's own teaching—was to accept what was offered, be thankful for it, but not to ask that anything be *killed for you*. This makes sense because if begging monks and nuns inspected the contents of their bowl and picked out and rejected what they didn't like, those who had offered what they could wouldn't feel encouraged to continue to give.

If it is ever necessary to kill to eat, the Buddhist does so with compassion. Thanking the bird or animal sharpens the awareness that this animal is a suffering sentient being, just as you are. Responsibility for your actions *always* lies with yourself in Buddhism.

Near the End

AFTER FORTY-FIVE years of traveling and teaching, the "Sage of the Sakya clan," as the Buddha became known, was an old man. His strength was failing, and his faithful attendant Ananda did all he could for his teacher's health and comfort. The Buddha died in Kusinara, surrounded by many of his *Sangha* members and followers. His body was cremated, and his ashes were divided to be interred in shrines around the country. Later, they were re-divided and further dispersed.

In the late nineteenth century, an urn bearing this inscription was found at Piprahwa in India:

This is the urn of the relics of the
Bhagavat, the Buddha of the Sakya tribe,
that is enshrined (by honorable brothers
and sisters, wives and children).

Kogen Mizuno, *The Beginnings of Buddhism*

Bhagavat means "sage" in Sanskrit, and "the Buddha of the Sakya tribe" is the title used to refer to Siddhartha Gautama during and after his lifetime. This urn is accepted as having been his family's share of the relics.

TWO

IS BUDDHISM A
RELIGION OR A PHILOSOPHY?

WHAT EXACTLY (OR as nearly as possible) is the definition of what we call Buddhism? Even to most of its adherents, it is popularly known as a religion. That being the case, what exactly (or as nearly as possible) is the definition of a religion?

According to *Webster's Dictionary*, a religion is "the service or adoration of God as expressed in forms of worship, in obedience to divine commandments and in pursuit of a way of life." Another dictionary defines religion as "belief in a supernatural power or powers, belief in a god or gods, especially such belief as entails acts of worship on the part of the believer; a developed system of philosophical, theological and ethical opinions, tenets and theories depending ultimately and essentially upon a belief in a deity or deities, and the necessity of worshipping that deity or those deities."

According to these definitions, it's understandable that popular Buddhism is seen as a religion. However, Buddhism does not teach that Buddha is God or even *a* god. The Buddha gave no commandments regarding service to or worship of himself. He was not, and did not claim to be, supernatural—he was a human being whose only difference from the human beings of today was cultural. Even that has not changed greatly in the area in which he lived.

The Buddha didn't teach religion. The Buddha didn't profess to be God, a god, or the prophet of a god. He didn't profess to have received enlightenment from gods or the messengers of a god. He didn't offer salvation to those who chose to listen to him or damnation to those who did not, or could not listen to him. He dealt only with reality and humanity as it is.

In an early teaching of the Buddha, there is a discourse on metaphysics. The Buddha says:

Monks, I will teach you everything. Listen to it. What, monks, is "everything"? Eye and material form, ear and sound, nose and odor, tongue and taste, body and tangible objects, mind and mental objects. These are called "everything." A person might say, "I will reject this 'everything' and proclaim another 'everything.'" He may certainly have a theory (of his own). But when questioned, he would not be able to answer and would, moreover, be subject to vexation. Why? Because it would not be within the range of experience.

For the Buddha, everything outside the range of experience was speculation. If people believed that countless reincarnations were necessary for enlightenment and spent time in speculation on this, they were wasting time. For those who sought enlightenment in this life, time was more precious.

Many Buddhists today accept the Buddha as a "savior" and pray to him as Christians would to Jesus, Hindus would to Hindu gods or Muslims would to Allah or the prophets.

So is Buddhism a religion? Yes, and no. Yes—devotion to the memory of the Buddha has brought a "Buddhist religion" into being in different cultural environments. No—basic Buddhism is a philosophy of morality, ethics and much more. Buddhism is not a religion unless you make it so because of your needs.

The religious adaptation of the basic teachings arises because every culture takes and modifies—for its own use—any new ideas. Any attempt to discover the Buddha's teachings requires an understanding that even before the Buddha's teaching left India, it had already absorbed many beliefs that were early Hindu, Vedic and Brahminic. Not everyone who followed the Buddha understood what he taught. Many interpreted the teachings through their previously held ideas. Some of the very early non-Buddhist inclusions were:

Reward and punishment after death

Hell, a place of endless darkness

Sacrifice to gods

Cosmology

Gifts to priests

Belief in gods

Belief in accumulating "merit" to offset the effects of
    "bad Karma" in future lives

The amount of so-called Buddhist teachings from earlier Indian belief systems that was incorporated after the death of Buddha Sakyamuni is quite staggering.

As the Dharma was introduced into other countries, it was always influenced by the previous religion and culture of those countries. Yet, the basic tenets have remained unchanged. Therefore, it helps to view Buddhism through the culture in which it is found. This, of course, applies to any of the world religions—Buddhism, Judaism, Christianity, Islam, animism and so on.

The early English and European translators of Buddhist texts often saw their own religion in what they understood as Buddhism. This reinforced their preconceptions that all religions were pretty much the same. They were right—except that they had mistaken a philosophy for a religion.

The advantage of this confusion is that Buddhism now has something to offer everyone, no matter whether your mind-set is devotional, investigative or a little of each, as is the case with most of us.

The first translations of Buddhist texts from Pali into English or other European languages caused more confusion than clarification. Buddhism was seen by the first translators of Buddhist texts as a gentle but rigid religion dominated by the monastic ideal, a sort of Christianity with a Buddha instead of a Christ figure. Certainly, this view represented one side of Buddhism, but it concentrated on the religion without the philosophy. It concentrated on the monastic rules and a sort of filing system of the Buddha's teachings called the *Abhidhamma* in Pali. These rules and teachings were deciphered by translators with a Christian mind-set, each of whom had a different level of understanding of the Pali and Sanskrit languages from which they were translating. As a result, the personal bias of the translator is often evident in his or her translation.

Siddhartha Gautama, "Sage of the Sakya clan," didn't set out to found a religion but to teach anyone who wanted to learn about the meaning of existence. He taught that the wisdom to live with the least suffering, disappointment and frustration comes from understanding. He didn't profess to know everything or to be able to fix all the problems occurring in the world. He was trying to demonstrate the best way to handle troubles—not to kick, scream and lash out at others but to see existence clearly, so we can find the most skillful way of living our lives.

Rules became necessary as more and more men and women

thronged permanently to live near the Buddha. The monastic tradition grew out of this original community of men and women around the Buddha. For example, when younger people began to flock to the new teacher, parents became alarmed that their families would be left without an heir (the first son of the first son), so there arose the rule that parental permission had to be obtained by the would-be monastic. When husbands and wives left their families to follow their teacher, it became necessary for men and women to have separate monasteries for the sake of study and peace. These are a few simple explanations of the beginnings of the main rules that now exist for monastics.

What does this have to do with one's preference for religion or philosophy? As you investigate the Buddha's Dharma you may seek religious answers to your questions. Or, if you aren't satisfied with the concepts of faith and tradition, you may seek philosophical reasons for what seem like the problems and difficulties of life and for the meaning—if any—of existence.

Of what possible relevance to modern society are the philosophical-ethical-moral teachings of a man who was born twenty-five hundred years ago? With so many different religions in the world today, what can Buddhism offer? With so many recipes for mental and physical self-improvement and therapy being offered to us every day, what is it about this ancient philosophy that even today draws people of different races and nationalities?

The answer is that there is still suffering, in spite of our technological advances. Everyone still experiences birth, old age, sickness, death, association with painful persons and conditions, separation from loved ones and pleasant conditions, not getting what one desires, grief and other forms of mental and physical suffering. These are all included in the Sanskrit word *dukha*, which means "the lack of *lasting* satisfaction," or "suffering." No one escapes this in his or her life. Each of us has to find a personal way to handle the lack of lasting satisfaction or suffering. We call this search "the pursuit of happiness."

Listening to the news for just one day is enough to show that most of humanity's solutions to suffering do not work. Often the solutions leave the original problem worse and create a few more to keep it company. There are a thousand grisly stories of efforts to do good going wrong. We don't see clearly the interconnectedness of phenomena. I can think of no worse way to start the day than to listen to the news! Our adrenalin output goes up and then it crashes. Result—a feeling of hopeless depression. Even if someone has a bright optimism, often it seems like a shield against panic, despair and their fear of being overwhelmed emotionally.

Established religions are losing followers from among the educated. People have lost faith in "faith" and faiths. Unfortunately, there is no instant universal cure for the problem of suffering. Even with all our similarities and interconnectedness, we are still individual bundles of energy with different psychological patterns, forever bumping up against one another, sometimes causing pleasure and sometimes causing pain.

The numbers of doubters, disbelievers, seekers after enlightenment, and the spiritually empty will increase with the progress of education and learning across the world today. Where do we turn for something that makes sense? Where do we turn for something that helps us to get the most out of life?

While morals and ethics appear to be less and less important to more and more people today, society makes more laws after the fact in its attempt to force people to act responsibly for their own sake as well as for society as a whole. This achieves *more* crime because now there are *more* laws to be broken. The more we stress the rights of the individual over the rights of society as a whole, the less awesome seems the law to the individual, and the less respect the individual feels for the authority of society. If laws stand in the way of individuals' perceived pleasures, then their wishes become more important.

In an ideal society, our *wishes* might work best instead of laws. Our need for laws might wither away if everyone accepted responsibility for their actions as well as their actions' outcomes, instead of expecting to be pulled out of difficulties by friends, relatives or the authority they despise. But an ideal society remains an *ideal*. Personal freedom means personal responsibility.

So here we are, stuck in a mess that seems to get progressively messier. What can we do? Where can we start? The Buddhist reply is to start right *here*, right *now,* and begin to study mind control. *Your* mind. *My* mind. This is not brainwashing, which is control by outside forces, but control from within oneself.

The Buddha liked to get to the root of whatever the problem might be. His aim was to show the sufferer the solution. When trying to solve our individual problems, we too need to get right down to basics. The basis of society's problems lies within each individual. Each can do something about the whole problem but not everything. No one person can save the planet. The place to begin is at the individual level. When we work at solving our own problems, we have already made a contribution to solving the problems around us.

WHAT ARE THE DIFFERENT KINDS OF BUDDHISM?

VERY BROADLY SPEAKING, there are today three main divisions of *religious* Buddhism. These are Theravada, Mahayana and Zen Buddhism. Each of these is divided further into sects, and these sects adhere to different interpretations of Buddhism by past and present teachers. These many divisions have arisen over twenty-five hundred years, and some are of long standing while others are relatively recent.

One of the three main divisions, *Theravada,* is generally known as the Southern School of teachings. It reached what was then called Ceylon during the reign of the Indian King Ashoka, in the third century B.C. The scriptural texts of the Southern School—its followers are called *Theravadins*—were recorded in the Pali language, in contrast to Northern School texts, which were recorded in Sanskrit. The first translations of Buddhist texts to reach the West were from the Pali or Southern School.

The second main division, *Mahayana,* is today the most widespread branch of Buddhist religion. It appears in China, Mongolia, Tibet, Vietnam, Japan and now Australia, North America and Europe. The main appeal of Mahayana lies in its belief in the *bodhisattva* ideal (*bodhisattva* means "awakened person," or "person with a noble heart," in Sanskrit). The *bodhisattva* is what Christians and possibly Muslims would call a *saint*—one who stands at the gates of paradise through a life purely lived and forgoes entry until every last being in the universe has passed through with the bodhisattva's help. In this context, Buddha Sakyamuni is the great, supreme bodhisattva.

The third main division, *zen,* spread from India to China, then to Japan and now to Australia and North America. It is considered to be a very direct path to enlightenment. Zen is also considered part of the *Mahayana* tradition. There is an *apparent* simplicity in Zen that appeals to those who love order and discipline. Zen is often thought of as a method of sudden enlightenment. This is incorrect. Sudden enlightenment can be attained only after acquiring much wisdom and knowledge. If you have no idea what you are aiming for, there can be no recognition of whatever it is you finally attain. Really, sudden enlightenment is a qualitative change after quantitative practice. This is similar to the bliss experienced on sudden resolution of a problem after we have worried ourselves sick over it and then flung it aside. Suddenly—there is the answer!

This sudden release of mental tension is not permanent. It is only a taste of the equanimity to come with true enlightenment.

Although there are these three great kinds of religious Buddhism today, Buddhism is not what Westerners think of as an *organized* religion. It has no pope, no archbishop, no bishop. Contrary to popular belief, His Holiness Tenzin Gyatso, the fourteenth Dalai Lama, is not the "Pope" of Buddhism. He is simply the most widely known Buddhist today. Every Buddhist country has its own most revered religious leaders, as does every group of students of religious Buddhism. *Guru, lama,* his holiness and similar names mean *teacher* or various gradations of reverence for a teacher. A teacher is the leader of a group of followers.

There is no authority on high passing down rules and regulations about the beliefs and practices of all Buddhists. There are new interpretations and new translations of Buddhist texts being presented almost regularly—this is the serious student's good fortune—but the basic teachings don't change.

Why Does Buddhism Have So Much Ritual?

I TEND TO believe that the Buddha taught a philosophy and not a religion. But then why has every sect of Buddhism developed so much ritual? The non-Buddhist who visits Buddhist centers is confronted by people behaving in strict ways. Events take place at prescribed hours, certain postures and gestures are used, certain words are chanted over and over—just as is done in the churches of other religions. Is this ritual necessary? What is the purpose of it all?

Ritual begins as a form of training. In Buddhism, ritual is for the purpose of concentrating mental attention on something other than our daily affairs. Everything the practitioner does during practice or on entering a shrine area is to further concentrate one's attention on the Dharma until every act of body, speech and mind serves the same purpose. This appears senseless and bewildering to the person visiting a Buddhist establishment out of mere curiosity. If you come seeking serenity, often you'll be confused by the noise of gongs, bells and drums.

As I've said, the purpose of ritual is for training. This applies to all human life. When we are infants, our parents train us by rituals of waking, washing, dressing and mealtimes. Breakfast, lunch and dinner are held at certain times, require clean hands and neat clothing, and usually mean sitting at a table with others. Ritual continues at school and in the workplace. Ritual has an important place in situations where many diverse personalities are thrown together and individual traits can become distracting. Also, rituals appeal to our sense of beauty and order. They can lift us out of ourselves to a higher plane of concentration. Trouble arises when rituals become rites. If rituals become the only way to keep the sky from falling on us, or the only way of avoiding disaster, rituals have become rites and superstition. Buddhist practice is not about rites. Adhering to rites for such reasons misses the point entirely.

We need to look carefully at the rituals of our lives to try to understand their original purpose. If we are open-minded, we should also refrain from prejudging the rituals of other groups. Even if they have become corrupted, there was once a purpose to them. If understood correctly, this purpose may still be of much use.

Is There a Heaven and Hell?

THERE ARE HEAVENS and hells for the religious Buddhist. These realms differ according to the pre-Buddhist beliefs of a given culture. In Tibetan Buddhist religious teachings there are three hot and three cold hells—all mental states—often accepted as fact by followers. There are said to be various heavenly realms that are wonderful—and impermanent. The hellish realms are as horrifying as imagination can make them—and they are also impermanent There is no *everlasting* glory, no *everlasting* torment, in Buddhism.

Let me relate an incident I witnessed some years ago. A visiting teacher came to a center where I was. He was a quite famous teacher of Tibetan Buddhism, a person of great wisdom and compassion and an outstanding scholar. He was teaching from Buddhist texts to an audience of monks, nuns, residents and visitors. When this is done in the West, the teacher reads what is written in the woodblock-printed text (original translations obtained from China and India when Buddhism was first introduced) and a translator translates his words. This teacher had read the text on the heavenly realms and now went on to the hells. A middle-aged couple who had spent every day of the seminar snorting cynically sat stiffly on chairs pushed as far back as the walls allowed.

A question period followed the reading, and as usual the teacher answered through his interpreter. Now the woman stood up and put her question *very* firmly: "Would the teacher kindly indicate to us the *exact geographical position* of these hell realms?"

He chuckled softly as the interpreter translated the question, then he replied. This was the translation: "The teacher says to ask you—where is your mind?" At this the lady and her husband stood up and stomped out of the center, slamming doors behind them. They packed their van and left that day. They thought they had been insulted! Heaven and hell are certainly in our minds. We are in heaven or hell almost every day of our lives. Heaven and hell are experienced in *this* life. If they are experienced elsewhere, well, we will find out—or we won't.

Not all Buddhists have the inclination or capability to *investigate* the philosophy on which their religion is built. Therefore, they tend to follow those teachings most acceptable to their beliefs. They offer prayers, carry out rituals, believe the historical stories and folktales they feel they should believe, and in this way they absorb into their lives whatever helps them to live the way they choose. There is no fault to be found in this, although there is the danger of accepting whatever we are told without vigorously investigating it for ourselves—as the Buddha advised.

What Happens When We Die?

THE BUDDHA NEVER gave answers to questions of this nature. Some people think that this means he taught there is *nothing* after what we call death. This is not correct. Instead, he discouraged idle speculation on this or any such subject. To those who speculated, he simply asked if anyone had returned to give them provable information. However, he *did* explain the doctrine of impermanence, constant change and flux—and these teachings apply to what we call death as well as to anything else.

Death is a suitable subject for meditation. Buddhists don't fear death, accepting its inevitability as part of the natural cycle of birth and death. We don't even know what death is, when it occurs, or at what exact point it is complete. When I was a young nurse, when a medical practitioner confirmed a death we straightened the body, tied up the jaw, and left the body undisturbed for one hour. Was this just to make sure? Or was this instinctive knowledge that the exact point of death is never clear?

For a Buddhist, death can't be the *end.* What we call death can't be a concrete, everlasting, unchanging event. For a Buddhist it can only be the end of one phase and a stage in becoming something else.

There are no *ends* in Buddhism. Ends imply beginnings. The Buddha taught impermanence, flux and constant change. Even the gaining of enlightenment is not an end but "No more of this state," as the Buddha said—an endless becoming, whatever that becoming may turn out to be. The idea of the beginning or end of a life-stream is impossible for a Buddhist. According to the Buddha's words,

[t]his cycle of continuity (this un-enlightenment) is without a visible end, and the first beginnings of beings wandering and running around, enveloped in ignorance and bound down by the fetters of thirst (desire) is not to be perceived. The first beginning of ignorance is not to be perceived in such a way as to postulate that there was no ignorance beyond a certain point.

The word *ignorance* in Buddhist teachings doesn't mean lack of knowledge, education or intelligence. It simply means lack of the inner wisdom that is full enlightenment. In Buddhism, it isn't possible to say that what we call life begins or ends. It makes no sense to a Buddhist to fear *inescapable* change. So there is no need for despair regarding the subject of eventual death—one's own or others'. Nothing lasts forever—not happiness or unhappiness. Enjoy the moment now, and accept that things will change.

One of the finest Buddhist parables is that of the young mother whose infant had died. She carried the body around begging for help, until the villagers sent her to the Buddha in the hope that he might cure her madness. The Buddha offered to help if she would leave the infant's body with his followers, go into the nearby town and collect a mustard seed from a dwelling in which no one had lost a loved one to death. She went with high hopes and returned with empty hands, having learned that no one escapes the sorrow of losing a loved one. She became one of the Buddha's followers.

What *is* it that continues in the continuity of becoming? Buddha taught that it is the thirst of *life force*, the desire for *continual becoming*—for another birth which will lead to another death, and so on. This desire ceases through wisdom, and this wisdom can be developed in this life. When the continual cycling through birth and death is overcome through wisdom, then future change can proceed in a different way.

One of the Buddha's disciples gave an interesting reply to the question, "Does a man live after death?" The reply was, "We do not know whether he is the body, or in the body, or other than the body whilst alive. How can we know whether, after the death of the body, he is dead?"

There is a phrase often used by the Buddha regarding release from the condition of ignorance. This phrase speaks of the fully awakened state, and it says, "What has to be done is done; there is no more to be done *on this account*." The last words in the phrase are often translated as "in this state." Whichever translation is used it is clear that there is no end, even for the fully enlightened one.

Whether you choose to accept belief in reincarnation where a being retains personal memory, belief in simple rebirth into another form without personal identity, or belief in the further becoming of whatever reality lies in the sentient being—in any of these beliefs, there is no end. No *event* goes on forever. No one is *forever* being born or *forever* dying. No one is *forever* a child, *forever* a mature adult or *forever* old. Even within these phases we are constantly changing. Only change continues.

In one of the early teachings, there is a list of subjects that the Buddha taught were only speculation, not matters of experience:

1. Did I exist in the past?
2. Did I not exist in the past?
3. What was I in the past?
4. How was I in the past?
5. Having been what, did I become what in the past?
6. Shall I exist in the future?
7. Shall I not exist in the future?
8. What shall I be in the future?
9. How shall I be in the future?
10. Having been what, shall I become what in the future?

Or regarding the present time:

11. Am I?
12. Am I not?
13. What am I?
14. How am I?
15. Whence came this person?
16. Whither will he go?

The Buddha said, when a person reflects unwisely in this way, one of the six false views arises:

1. I have a Self: this view arises in him as true and real.
2. I have no Self: this view arises in him as true and real.
3. By Self I perceive Self: this view arises in him as true and real.
4. By Self I perceive non-Self: this view arises in him as true and real.
5. By non-Self I perceive Self: this view arises in him as true and real.
6. Or a wrong view arises in him as follows: This is my Self, which speaks and feels, which experiences the fruits (outcomes) of good and bad actions now here and now there. This Self is permanent, stable, everlasting, unchanging, remaining the same forever and ever.

Walpola Rahula, *What the Buddha Taught*

These views, seen as true and real, are false. This is another instance of the Buddha's advice not to waste time trying to solve the unsolvable.

Quantum science says that what continues can only be ever changing patterns of probability, activity that can't be predicted. In other words, *anything* could happen. Trying to predict the unpredictable is not conducive to gaining real knowledge. Here science and Buddha Sakyamuni are in full agreement, as in so many other instances.

Buddhism accepts that none of us knows the exact hour of our death, not even if we have been sentenced to death judicially or if we are terminally ill. Most of us deliberately or subconsciously ignore the subject of death altogether although friends, relatives and strangers are dying around us at every moment. Death seems to be some strange but quite natural phenomenon that will and does happen to other people—not to us. Others see death as the only way out of unhappiness and suffering.

For most of us, the fear is not of death per se, because common sense tells us we can't avoid it no matter how hard we fight it, but of the *manner* of our death. Will we die alone and lonely, or in dreadful pain with loss of all dignity? Will we be so afraid that our dying hours become hours of terror, fearful of what is seen as the approaching annihilation of the self? It is the *dying*, not the death, everyone worries about, whether they expect there to be a heaven "on the other side" or not.

The Buddhist attitude is that, in order to have a peaceful death, we need to practice having a peaceful life, to live each day as though it were the last. Leave no animosity, resentment, vengeful thoughts, unpaid emotional debts, regrets or unresolved misunderstandings at the day's end. Behave as though reward and punishment really are a part of the after-death experience and be prepared. In this way, the mind will be calm and peaceful at all times even if death comes sooner than expected.

The other side of this practice is that if we ourselves have a calm and peaceful attitude toward death and dying, we can be of great help to those who know they are dying now. By being prepared for death, you do away with humanity's greatest fear, and you are able to help others at *their* time of greatest need. This may sound depressing, but look at the Buddhists you know. Are they constantly miserable and gloomy? Not at all.

THREE

PART I

WHAT DID
THE BUDDHA TEACH?

*W*HAT WAS IT that this man considered worth trying to teach to those who wanted to listen? As far as we have been able to discover, here are the main earliest teachings of the Buddha. There are no divine commandments, no threat of eternal damnation, no promises of a perfect happy ending. Instead, he gave moral and ethical advice and explanations of action and reaction (*karma*).

The teachings that the Buddha gave to his very first listeners seem to have been on *impermanence* and the *emptiness of inherent existence of all compound phenomena*. These are a little difficult to begin with—his earliest listeners were already advanced philosophers and yogis—so I will discuss these teachings in the following section. First, I'd like to begin with the Buddha's teaching on the *Four Noble Truths* (better translated as "truths of the Noble Ones") and the *Eightfold Path* of conduct.

THE FIRST NOBLE TRUTH

THE *FIRST NOBLE Truth* is the truth of *dukha.* This Sanskrit term is usually translated as suffering, but this is not quite what the Buddha meant. He had a wider view of suffering that included ideas such as imperfection, impermanence and insubstantiality. His notion of suffering really connotes the meaning of lacking in *lasting* satisfaction. This is because of the Buddha's teaching on *impermanence.*

There is no one word to translate the whole concept of suffering. The truth of suffering is not getting what we want and having to suffer what we don't want. It is also birth, old age, sickness, death, sadness, grief, association with the unpleasant, separation from the pleasant, the ungraspable quality of phenomena and all forms of mental and physical sufferings of existence. No matter how fortunate we are in worldly goods, health, fame and talent, we can never escape the truth of suffering. Our existence *is* suffering. Suffering *is* our existence.

This seems obvious the longer one is alive, yet most people in every new generation never consider this. Never. They talk about their own particular luck, fate, "karma," genetics and how they were brought up, but they can't see that their suffering is the same for everyone.

To acknowledge the natural existence of suffering undermines self-pity. Suffering isn't just *my* fate. It is *everyone's* fate. No one escapes it. The most saintly person experiences suffering. The richest and poorest human beings in the world can't possibly escape suffering. The healthiest creature, living in the most ideal conditions, is subject to suffering.

The first step on the path to freedom from suffering is to become truly *aware* of suffering. Don't hide from truth and pretend it isn't so. No one of us can cure a condition unless we acknowledge it first.

The next step on the path to freedom from suffering is the *wish* to be free from suffering. Impermanence is change that alters a situation, so it also alters situations we'd like to escape. But this doesn't happen in an orderly pattern. There are countless patterns developing and declining in an interconnected manner all the time. For someone with no conception of this aspect of real life, the result is confusion, frustration or some degree of moral or mental breakdown. One would imagine most beings would wish to be free of such confusion, frustration and suffering, but there are millions, if not billions, who don't. Even though we see others who appear to have accepted life as it is and act accordingly, we don't ask ourselves why they are able to do this. We see only our own condition. "Life seems so unfair. Why do *I* deserve this cruel fate? Why should *some* people have everything? What is the *reason* for it all?"

The Second Noble Truth

THE BUDDHA WENT into great detail to explain the cause of suffering because a problem cannot be corrected unless we find the cause. We can participate in distracting indulgences or in self-denial and rituals, but these only alleviate suffering momentarily. They don't cure whatever is causing it. Hard work and personal honesty are required in order to discover the cause of our suffering.

The Buddha's *Second Noble Truth* states that there is a cause of suffering—it is craving, wanting or *desirousness*.

From a single cell on, all life seeks to be safe and comfortable rather than remain in discomfort. When we find what seems to bring us happiness, we cling to it and crave more of it. This desirousness is needed initially for our survival as human beings. Without it we would perish as babies. But once we have become independent beings, craving isn't necessary to the same degree, and it becomes the cause of suffering.

CRAVING

This desirousness isn't the same as wanting something that is possible or needed. It is craving for the *impossible*, or for what is impossible *for us* as particular individuals. Who on a limited income doesn't sometimes want great wealth? What plain man or woman doesn't want a beautiful face? We are never satisfied. No amount of wealth, beauty or love is ever enough. We ignore what we *do* have in our craving for what we *don't* have, and we often crave what is impossible for us to *ever* have. It is sensible to want what we need, but it is a source of suffering to crave the unattainable.

Craving is a wish to possess wholly, to cling to. When we crave to have something, we want it to remain as it is at that moment. We want to be able to *have* our cake and enjoy eating it. We want the person we love *never* to change. We want death to be suspended for us and for our family. We cannot accept the other teaching of the Buddha—impermanence. Absolutely nothing remains the same for as long as a snap of the fingers. We can't accept this fact, and we equate impermanence with suffering. But *all* compounded phenomena—all phenomena made up of other phenomena—are subject to change. The body I was born with isn't the body I have today. The river I step into this morning won't be the same river this evening—or even one second from now.

Clinging, craving and the expectation of permanence are the cause of suffering. Clinging to concepts and opinions is also a cause of violence. People talk about principles which we will kill or die for. Often these principles are badly flawed, but we never admit that possibility. Anyone who has different principles becomes our enemy automatically. We stand by our principles to the death—preferably, the death of others.

We find the perfect partner, and life is sweet and satisfying. The partner changes (for a variety of reasons) and we are in hell on earth, forgetting that we too have changed. Parents delight in the babyhood of their child. They think they know all there is to know about this person; and they suffer as the child changes, disagrees with them, and one day gladly leaves them.

We live in a place where we have known only happiness and a feeling of security, only to be suddenly uprooted because of economic or environmental changes. We lose our photos and knick-knacks because of flood or fire. On top of this, we lose a loved one. And after everything is gone, we mentally cling to our memories as something concrete and real and in this way prolong our grief.

Nothing can make us joyful in the face of sorrow, but if we are *aware* of the truth of impermanence, we can reduce the pain. We can discover that craving and clinging are the cause of pain more than the loss itself.

The most damaging part of craving and clinging may be that they rule out investigation or analysis of a situation. They preclude our seeing things as they really are (or as near as possible), and so they stop us from acting skillfully. With clear thinking our skillful action may lead to a solution of the problem. If there is no solution, at least we will be able to accept the present condition and go on to something better than pain or anger, refusing to accept personal responsibility, and suffering.

A mind free of clinging and craving is a mind free of worry. A mind free of worry is able to concentrate fully on the task at hand. A mind free of worry is able to expand beyond petty and imaginary problems. Such a mind knows it isn't what happens to us that is of prime importance, but how we react to what happens to us. If our mind is busy clinging and craving and worrying about what we call security, our reactions won't be skillful and the outcome of our actions won't be what we hoped for.

GREED, HATRED AND IGNORANCE

THE BUDDHA TALKED about greed, hatred and ignorance, or the pain of passion, aggression and ignorance. We all suffer from the conditions of greed or passion, hatred or aggression, and especially ignorance. These are also the cause of suffering, the Second Noble Truth. The teaching on these three is one of the most basic Buddhist teachings. Every practicing Buddhist attempts to control their own greed, hatred and ignorance.

Of course, at this moment each one of us knows for sure that we are *not* greedy, we do *not* hate anyone enough to want to thump them, and as for ignorance—how dare anyone cast such a slur on us. We are educated, thinking beings!

Before you begin to feel insulted, let me explain what is meant in the context of Buddhist teaching regarding these three words.

GREED

The original word translated as passion or greed is *desirousness,* as I mentioned. Desirousness is not simply *desire,* but that particular *grasping* kind of want or need with which we are born and without which we wouldn't survive.

Desirousness is appropriate for infants who grasp at anything they can get their hands and mouths on. Everything they hold or see is theirs. But we continue to be *inappropriately* possessive as adults. We may throw spectacular tantrums when we can't have it all and then suffer enormously, and cause others to suffer too. Even when we *do* get what we want, we still suffer unless we understand the truth of impermanence, change and constant flux. Our newest, most costly car will deteriorate. Our new house won't stay new forever. Our present love affair—the one to end all love affairs—will change. Our babies will become restless teenagers, and the ones we love will go away or become sick, die and leave us.

If we don't understand and *accept* that everything is changing from moment to moment, that nothing can remain the same for even one snap of our fingers, we will try to cling to something that has no *inherent* existence—and we will experience suffering. Throwing tantrums, getting drunk or stoned, hitting someone or something, screaming and smashing things, or even killing won't make the slightest difference except to produce more suffering for ourselves and others. Even in the face of inevitable death we may add to our suffering—still craving and clinging for existence as we think we understand it to be.

Greed refers to this grasping kind of craving and clinging. It includes covetousness, envy and jealousy. It is the irrational craving for what can't possibly be obtained by the sufferer—either because of lack of capability, because of lack of ability to see opportunity when it arises, or because the object of desire belongs to someone else, or in some way is completely out of the sufferer's reach. Greed *is* suffering. Even if satisfied for a short time, greed leads to lack of *lasting* satisfaction. Overindulgence leads to revulsion, but we are slow to learn. As soon as saturation is achieved, we immediately change the focus of our craving. Grand passions usually end in tragedy. Passionate desire deteriorates after thirty years into petty family feuds.

Greed can almost be said to be the natural condition of all that lives, because we are born in a state of *desirousness*. At first, greed is instinctive and necessary because without the desire for food we would die. But as the intellect develops, greed remains as strong as ever. In this permanent state of desirousness, our attention is captured by something—we are attracted to *it, him* or *her*—and immediately our desire is transferred to it or them. The object may be a person, animal, jewels, a building, a car, a landscape or whatever. And now the problem of desire is compounded by the expectation that the desired object will never change in any way from our concept of its reality!

Clinging is part of greed. Greed says, "What is mine is mine, and what is yours is mine," and clinging adds, "I am not going to give it back, and I want more of it." The more we cling to our ideas, opinions, material possessions, mistaken memories and emotional relationships, the greater our distress when change becomes apparent. To lose what is possessed, or to have our prized opinions and concepts proven wrong, is painful in proportion to the strength with which we cling to them.

Is greed simply eating too much at dinnertime, or drinking until we are incapably drunk? The greed I am talking about is really an attitude of mind—*a grasping attachment.* In itself, greed causes hatred and is caused by ignorance.

HATRED

Hatred or *aggression* is another source of suffering because it destroys the hater's mind. Perhaps this word is better translated as *aversion*—not wanting any association whatever with what is not pleasing. Hatred isn't always extreme or obvious. As with any emotion, there are degrees. At one end of the scale of aversion, hatred is distaste. At the other end of the scale, hatred can be murderous intent.

If we can recognize the weaker forms, it is easier to control the emotion before it takes over completely. Instead, we love and cling to all our emotions—even misery—and are afraid to relinquish them. No matter what we suffer through our emotions, at least they prove us to be what we consider alive. But this isn't so. We don't live fully until we stop reacting to life through the veil of our emotions. Emotion is another word for the high's and low's of attachment and aversion, love and hate. When we can love without emotion—a balanced, even love—we have achieved the Buddha's universal compassion, loving everyone equally and unconditionally.

Hatred is really *excessive aversion*. We hate what is foreign to our way of seeing things. We fear what we don't understand, and what we fear we either run away from or seek to destroy. So-called "holy" wars (a contradiction in terms) are caused by strong aversion to something *other*. This is often something not understood, which arouses a subconscious fear—for example, fear of God's wrath because of the existence of unbelievers, or fear that other views may threaten the truth of our own beliefs, which we want to see as the only *real* truths. Anger is part of hatred, too—a slightly milder form, but having the potential to develop quickly into full-blown hatred. Anger is a cause of suffering to ourselves first of all. No one can be joyful or kind while being angry. Anger eats into us—mentally and physically—like acid. Anger needs to be considered carefully because of its potential for damage to ourselves and others, and because of the long-lasting consequences of its effects.

There is a Buddhist practice that helps overcome anger and hatred. This is to analyze *the feeling itself* while it is happening, *the actual physical feeling*—the way we seem to swell with anger, like a cat raising every hair on its end, the feeling of our face burning, our heart racing, the feeling in our throat of literally choking with rage. We tremble with the force of our emotion. The Buddhist idea is to make us fully aware of what is going on *within ourselves*. As we investigate our own feelings, we slow down; and the next step becomes possible. This next step is asking ourselves, "What is the *real* cause of my anger?" Quite often it turns out to be nothing more than a bruised ego, or it is caused by a deep-seated fear.

Then we need to consider our own part in the situation very honestly. This isn't taking time to hand out blame. No judgment is being made. We are merely seeking clarity. Although there is no such thing as a simple cause and effect, simplifying the picture helps us to see a little more clearly that we are, in part, responsible for this distressing emotion. No one can *make* me angry—I *choose* to respond to a certain event by becoming angry. I am in charge of my own emotions. In all fairness, I can't blame another person because of *my* emotional responses. Statements such as, "*You* made me angry," "*You* make me so happy," "*You* ruined my life," and so on are made from not understanding the situation.

It takes less effort and feels more satisfying to attribute the cause to someone or something other than ourselves. But accepting responsibility for our own contribution to situations increases our self-respect and control over our own lives and gives awareness that we are not powerless—ever.

This Buddhist practice isn't easy. First, we explore deeply the reasons for our hatred. Sometimes we hate in another person what we see or are afraid of developing in ourselves. Sometimes we hate because we don't understand, or we are mistaken. Sometimes we hate because our beliefs are challenged, and we know we are unable to uphold them. Sometimes we allow ourselves to be humiliated, and then we seek revenge. All this has searing effects on character, but these effects can be overcome.

Another method for overcoming hatred is based on the mental practice of exchanging oneself for others. Using a belief in reincarnation, this states that if we have lived countless lives, and if we will reincarnate countless more times, then we have all had a different social status and even a different sex. And at some time the enemy we have today has been our loving mother or father, sister or brother, husband or wife, child or lover. The person we love today has at one time been an enemy, and the person we are indifferent to today has been any or all of the above.

The practice itself involves quiet meditation. Imagine a loved one to your right, the one you hate to your left, and the person you feel neutral about in front. Then begin to mentally exchange one for the other and for oneself. Do this until the futility of clinging to your hatred becomes apparent. Next time you are confronted with what you hate, recognize the insubstantiality of your hatred and the loving kindness you have shared in past lives. Your excessive aversion will subside. If your hatred began because of an injury done to you, it is overcome by compassion for the injurer, whom you now see as a person who is like yourself—suffering.

This practice is not a matter of being wishy-washy or sentimental. It is a matter of fully understanding the situation in the widest sense possible. We come to see another being as a suffering sentient being like ourselves. And we forgive ourselves for being ignorant not to have seen this sooner. Forgiveness is a letting go of resentment and blame. We aren't ignoring the situation. We are understanding it.

IGNORANCE

As this word is used in Buddhism, ignorance is ignorance of *the way things really are* at this moment, ignorance of *right knowledge*. Ignorance is simply *not knowing*. This ignorance is the cause of unfortunate mistakes. It is as though we had arrived in a country where we were completely ignorant of the laws, language and terrain. In this situation, our best intentions would have the most unfortunate consequences.

Ignorance implies *not knowing*, confusion, not being aware of the way phenomena actually exist, and therefore, of why things are the way they have become. This is not a slur on one's intelligence or education—it is simply the state of being unaware of the illusory nature of existence.

This also implies ignorance of the difference between skillful and unskillful behavior. Buddhism stresses the importance of our motive. We need to be constantly aware of our motives for a certain course of action. If our motive is right, then usually the outcome is, too.

Of course, to excuse a disastrous outcome on the grounds that we "meant well" is questionable. If we are generous with the hope of reward, or kind with the hope of a good reputation, again our motive is questionable. Giving needs to be giving for its own sake, and kindness needs to be given with no attachment to receiving thanks or recognition as a benefactor.

Would any of us behave in an unskillful, harmful way if we knew for sure that it would have an adverse effect? In our *ignorance* of cause and effect and impermanence, we continue to act in unskillful ways over and over again.

KARMA, OR CAUSE AND EFFECT

"If I move a grain of sand, I change the universe." Think of this for a moment. Try to view this image as if you stood outside the universe and time passed as in a sped-up film. A grain of sand is moved, which causes another grain to shift a fraction, and another, and so on, without ceasing. Imagine the grain of sand that moves as your motives and actions. That is *karma*—the reason why things are the way they are at any given moment. Your karma, my karma, everybody's karma. Karma is not something we will experience at some other time in the form of punishment and reward. It is the *accumulated effect of actions.* From ignorant unskillful action comes what we call *bad karma* and from skillful action comes what we call *good karma.* At this very moment, we are the product of past *karma* or action, and what we are doing now is the seed of future karma or action.

Be careful of your motives for any given action!

Buddhism stresses awareness of the actions of our body, speech and mind. We can use our body to do great harm or we can use it skillfully. We can use our speech for harm, to slander, insult, insinuate or humiliate, or we can speak only kindly, truthfully and not indulge in gossip.

As to the mind, the mind *drives* the body. The Buddha reminded his followers that *where the mind goes with attachment, the body goes.* A mind full of lust leads to desire and action to possess the body or property of another person. Cruel thoughts are fore-runners of cruel actions. Erroneous thoughts lead to unskillful reactions to circumstances. That person aware of body, speech and mind works to keep his or her mind in wholesome channels, avoiding unkind, lustful or destructive thoughts.

The Third Noble Truth

OH, DOOM! OH, gloom! Isn't Buddhism a woeful philosophy, just as you always knew it was? But wait! There is more!

The Buddha did not teach that *everything* is suffering. He did not deny the existence of beauty and joy. He taught that *this* is suffering—our everyday existence. His aim in teaching us was to show us how to be happy right now and in the very next moment of *this* existence. This is the *Third Noble Truth*—freedom from suffering.

If it weren't for a third noble truth, we'd create a god or demon and blame our suffering on that. Instead, the Third Noble Truth tells us there is a way out of our craving and clinging, a way out of our greed, hatred and ignorance and consequent suffering. It tells us there is a way to live a happier life and be more successful in what we undertake to achieve.

This third truth simply states—there *is* a way out of suffering. It is not won through rites, rituals or submission to superstition. The way out of the effects of suffering begins the very moment we become *truly aware* of the real condition of existence. This awareness may begin as a momentary spark, which just as suddenly may be gone. But once this awareness is experienced, it will happen again.

If it's true that people believe only what they want to believe, then the world is full of people who prefer suffering. Yet there's such a simple remedy for beginning the healing process of the Third Noble Truth:

Enjoy what you have now but accept that it is already changing.
Do no harm to living beings, including yourself.
Learn to control your mind by being aware of things as they really are, now.

The Fourth Noble Truth

THE *FOURTH NOBLE Truth* presents an eightfold path as the way out of suffering. The Buddha's *Eightfold Path* was taught in several different ways, depending on the philosophical level of the hearer, but the basic steps remain the same. The path is excellent material to meditate on. It can have a different meaning for different people, but there is no great difficulty involved in following this Eightfold Path. The difficulty is in deciding to do so.

These are the eight ideas of the Path, which the Buddha advised to cultivate:

1. *Right views or understanding free from superstition.* This is not necessarily a religious attitude. It is clear thinking and common sense, free from the tainting influence of emotion.

2. *Right aims, high and worthy of an intelligent and earnest person.* Well, you wouldn't be reading this book if your aims were low and wicked, would you? Often we're interested in Buddhism because we aspire to something better than desperately scrambling for all we can get out of life, no matter whom we hurt in the process.

3. *Right speech or speech that is kind, open and truthful.* Before we speak, we should ask ourselves, is it necessary? Is it true? Is it kind? In childhood most of us learned the saying, "If you can't say something nice, don't say anything at all." We've all been hurt by words at one time or another, and we've all said hurtful things. Sometimes we justify our words saying, "Well, it's the truth." It may seem to be true, but is

it kind or necessary? And how sure can we be that it is true, anyway?

4. *Right action or right conduct in all aspects of life.* This is certainly the aim of most of us, but do we always investigate honestly the ethics of what we do? Sometimes it seems that if we shut our eyes to ethics, we will gain an advantage. If we consciously know our action is unethical and still go ahead, at the very least we'll suffer from a bad conscience. If we pretend to ourselves the act isn't unethical, we will still suffer— our subconscious will see to that!

5. *Right livelihood or doing no harm to sentient beings.* Once upon a time this was easy—don't kill or harm any form of life if you can avoid it. But in today's world, how on earth are we going to find work that does no harm to life? We can say no to working in slaughterhouses. We can say no to working in laboratories where animals are used in experiments that harm them. We can say no to working in munitions factories and factories geared to chemical warfare on humans and insects. But almost every other way of earning a living involves harm to life in some way. Even nursing the sick involves polluting the air and waters with chemical disinfectants. All we can do is keep our motives pure and do the best we can, wherever we may be.

6. *Right perseverance in all steps of the path.* This stands to reason. There's not much use beginning anything if we don't mean to persevere. Flitting from one philosophy or religion to another is wasting precious time, as is following only a few of these eight ideas—although I suppose, even taking on a few of these ideas is better than not following any of them at all!

7. *Right mindfulness or a watchful attentive mind that isn't easily distracted.* This can be a difficult idea for Westerners. There are so many distractions in our society—daily news, even hourly news, advertising, entertainment, elections, asserting our identity, making sure others know how clever and successful we are. Just one person can have all of these distractions—and more. There are people whose whole mental lives seem to consist of news, television stories, contests and the messages of glossy magazines. They don't realize how unaware they are of what they are really doing or what is really going on around them. Our own thoughts go around and around until our mind is a chaotic whirlpool and we long for peace. Buddhist teaching suggests we do something about this chaos before we break down.

8. *Right contemplation (meditation) or earnest reflection on the deep matters of life.* How often do any of us stop to think about what we're doing, what we're aiming for,

and how best to go about it? Many of us don't even want to think. We float on from moment to moment without contemplation, giving no thought to possibilities, letting ourselves be carried along into dangerous waters that could have been avoided. We give no thought to the possible outcome of mindless actions, and then we weep for the sorrows that overtake us. We hurt people we never meant to hurt. We make enemies without knowing why. Our business affairs and family life go kaput. We find ourselves in real trouble that we should have seen coming and could have prevented. Buddhist teaching is aimed to help us see the reality of our existence more clearly and in this way to avoid many of the pitfalls that might be encountered.

These eight steps are not rules, regulations or commandments. They are guidelines for beginning a life free from unnecessary suffering.

The Buddha also taught Five Precepts.

1. No lying
2. No stealing or taking what isn't offered
3. No killing
4. No unnatural sexual activity

5. No intoxication (by drugs, drink, and so on), which
   dulls the mind and makes one foolish

Again, these are guidelines for a life free from suffering. The
main purpose of the Buddha's teaching was to help sentient
beings—us—to live happier lives by *understanding*, not by obey-
ing rules or believing that help comes from "out there" or "up
there" somewhere. The four truths, the path and the precepts are
all simply *advice.* We can take the advice or we can ignore it—
and accept our part in the consequences.

The Four Noble Truths, the Eightfold Path and the Five
Precepts are the beginning of Buddha's teachings. They are the
foundation on which the rest of Buddhist teaching depends, and
they are teachings that can help us all, every day. They are teachings that are contemplated as part of *right contemplation,* the eighth
step on the Eightfold Path. Within them are two other simple but
profound teachings—impermanence and dependent-arising.

Dependent-arising is the concept that all things are connected.
Nothing emerges without relationship to other things. No
"thing" exists inherently, on its own. Everything is connected to
and influenced by everything else. A tree does not suddenly come
into existence, complete and entire. Your car didn't suddenly exist
out of nothing. A horse doesn't suddenly exist out of nothing. No
thing, natural or manufactured, exists out of nothing. This is what
Buddhists mean when they say no thing exists inherently

Impermanence, another profound Buddhist teaching, simply

means constant change. We are changing, and everything else is changing. Everything is in a constant state of flux. No thing either comes suddenly into being of its own accord, or remains the same, even for an instant.

Every cell in our bodies is constantly in a state of flux. Our thoughts are constantly changing. Our emotions are constantly changing. Our likes, dislikes, opinions and memories are changing. It is difficult to fully grasp this process of change because the rates of change of different things and different people are not uniform. Some changes we scarcely notice over the course of a century, like the weathering of the pyramids. Others we are aware of immediately, like our ever changing thoughts.

There are two more important teachings that are connected to these, and which are contemplated in the eighth step on the Path—right contemplation on *no self* and *no soul*.

The best way to understand *no self* is to recognize that what we call "the self" really isn't the way we are accustomed to perceiving it. This is simply because all the parts we think of as making up our self are constantly changing. There is nothing we can grasp at or hold onto because our self has already changed from the previous moment. Minutely, yes, but definitely changed. There is no self to grasp at, nothing to cling to, because everything changes from moment to moment. This is the truth of impermanence. Yet we continually try to stop change, and we suffer when we can't. How much better it is to see more clearly the way things really work!

Another important teaching to contemplate in right contemplation is *no soul*. *Soul* is something people hold to be eternal and unchanging, but how could this be so? There can be no such *thing*—no permanent concrete entity underlying our life. You don't have to believe this, but it is worth contemplating as the path suggests!

These Four Noble Truths, the Path and the Five Precepts, dependent-arising, impermanence, no self and no soul are very basic teachings of the Buddha. Simply reading about them will not bring about realization. That is why meditation is taught, so you can give all of your attention to whatever matter you have at hand. For Buddhists' peace of mind, future happiness and usefulness depend on taking these thoughts seriously —they are deep truths of our lives.

There is no concept of sin in Buddhism. Instead, there is ignorance of what is skillful or unskillful behavior. Following the Eightfold Path and living by the Five Precepts is skillful behavior. Doing harm to others or the environment and ignoring cause and effect (karma) is unskillful behavior.

Since there are no commandments to follow, the responsibility for our choice of behavior is entirely personal. Consciously or otherwise we choose the direction our steps will take. As Buddha said, *we go where our minds go*. If we let our mind dwell on flawed concepts and ill-considered, hard-held opinions, conflicts with others will soon arise. These conflicts will be followed by unskillful actions that call for more of the same on both sides.

The Buddha also taught ten factors that hold us back from reaching enlightenment—ten "fetters" that keep us locked in unskillful behavior. These are:

1. Belief in an inherently, permanently existing self
2. Skepticism about the impact of these ten factors
3. Belief in reaching enlightenment through rules and rites
4. Sensual lust (for whatever we desire)
5. Ill-will
6. Craving for a rich material existence
7. Craving for a rich *immaterial* existence.
8. Conceit
9. Restlessness
10. Ignorance

In Buddhist literature, there are many numbered lists because lists are easy to remember and repeat. Another list that relates to the truth of the path, or to *applying* what we understand, is called the *Seven Jewels of the Awakened Ones*. It lists the resources ("jewels") you will have when you are truly walking on the Buddhist path:

1. Full trust in the *Buddha,* the *Dharma* and the *Sangha*
2. Pure morality
3. Generosity
4. Right knowledge

5. Industriousness
6. Self-restraint that is aware of social and environmental considerations
7. Conscientious conduct

Although it may not seem obvious, no Buddhist, whether religious or nonreligious, is expected to be a meek and mild goody-goody. Buddhists aren't expected to be punching bags for belligerent people, or to stand silently when they are wrongfully accused. If a Buddhist remains silent under such treatment, it would only be because such behavior seemed *the most skillful* under the circumstances. Buddhism is not a matter of peace at all costs, but of wishing to *cause no harm to anyone.* There is a time to appear wrathful if this seems the best way to act in given circumstances. What is important is the motive for one's choice of action. You are not wrathful out of anger and hatred but out of compassion.

LOVING KINDNESS AND COMPASSION

FOLLOWING THE BUDDHA'S way and studying the Dharma (the Buddha's teachings) is meant to develop sympathetic understanding, gentleness and the ability to see the reasons for another's behavior. If you did no more than act with real compassion in every situation, you would almost be a Buddha. The sincere practice of *universal compassion* leads to enlightenment. A mind set on this path seeks to see clearly what needs to be done—or not done—and the best and most compassionate way to go about it. Seeing *clearly* is the way.

Having loving kindness and compassion doesn't mean that you throw your arms around a Hitler, child molester or rapist. Universal compassion doesn't require that you pat hungry and unhappy wild animals or make room for poisonous spiders in your house. It doesn't even require you to weep over an obnoxious neighbor or show them the error of their ways to save them.

It means you are aware that here, too, is a sentient being suffering from ignorance. It may not be your place to do anything, yet even while keeping your distance from a criminal, you acknowledge that he or she—along with all sentient beings—experiences suffering. In that we are *all* brothers and sisters.

Universal compassion means awareness at all times that *all sentient beings*—all things that live—experience suffering. Awareness of *universal suffering* is the first step toward *universal compassion*.

Thinking is a very rare activity. Thinking is what the Buddha tried to teach, thinking about existence—not in the manner of worrying and speculating but of being *fully aware of the way things have become in any given moment*.

Buddha didn't want people to have faith in what he said simply because he was awakened, or to believe what he told them without thinking about it for themselves.

When something happens to us—an event, something with which we are personally concerned, the Buddha said to consider how the present situation *arose* instead of reacting blindly out of greed, hatred, ignorance or fear. In other words, *think* about it, be as *aware* as possible of the causes and implications, and make sure our reactions are appropriate and useful.

FOUR

PART II

WHAT DID
THE BUDDHA TEACH?

$\mathcal{T}$HE BUDDHIST TEACHING that puzzles even Buddhists when they think about it is the doctrine of *no self,* which is also called the teaching on *emptiness.* Let me try to explain the Buddha's teachings on *no self* and *emptiness.* Once the core of the Buddha's teaching on *no self* and *emptiness* is understood, these words will have served their purpose—the journey then becomes an inner one of personal experience.

KARMA, REINCARNATION AND REBIRTH

FIRST LET'S LOOK more deeply at three concepts—karma, reincarnation and rebirth. Although they have different meanings, these three words are so entwined in the average Buddhist and non-Buddhist mind that they must be considered in their inter-connectedness. Understanding them will help us begin to understand what the Buddha meant by no self.

Karma means "action" in Sanskrit, and the Buddha used this definition. To begin with, action means *cause and effect*. For example, if you waste your money, you will experience a result of debt and poverty. If you are careless with guns and sharp instruments, you will harm yourself and others. If you insult someone grievously, you will lose a friend or make an enemy. If excessive rain falls in a ditch, there will be flooding. Simple cause and effect.

Of course, action is more than a case of "I do this and that happens," because there is much more going on in existence than what *you* do. *All* phenomena are compounded or made up of other phenomena. In this way, all phenomena are interdependent and interconnected. All phenomena are made up of many other phenomena, many other causes, conditions and effects. What goes on in one place affects what goes on in another place, no matter how minute the effect. This is *karma* to the Buddhist.

As for *reincarnation,* if your religion teaches reincarnation of the individual self, as pre- and non-Buddhist Indian and Asian religions did (and as most religious groups, including Christian, did in one way or another throughout their history), it seems evident to believers that when one reincarnates there will be delayed debts to pay and delayed rewards to receive. Presto!

Action and reaction (the Buddhist notion of karma) becomes karma as *punishment and reward, heaven and hell.* But the Buddha taught karma as a natural, non-judgmental action and reaction— not as punishment and reward.

Finally, *rebirth* is a word often mistaken to mean reincarnation. This is a natural misunderstanding coming from lack of reflection. One view of rebirth points to nature and the seasons. Someone could say that what "dies" in one season is "reborn" in another. The elements of the physical body "die" and are "reborn" as trees, grass and flowers. The energy of mind or soul or spirit leaves one plane of existence and comes into being again or proceeds to another plane.

Now, remember that the Buddha never entered the debate about whether or not there is something more after death. Instead of teaching about rebirth and reincarnation, he taught about *no self,* and he put the question like this.

Since there is no inherently permanent self, only a constantly changing physical, emotional or mental state, what is reborn?

When asking questions of this nature, he often pointed to a shady tree and suggested that the listener sit in the shade and think about the question from every angle. In other words, he asked the questioner to *meditate* on it. For the Buddhist what we call death is a momentary phenomenon—not an end, but part of ongoing existence. There is no actual *moment* of death as such— no *moment* that is an *end.*

GOD AND THE SOUL

WHAT, THEN, SHALL we make of God and the soul?

First, the assumption of a "creator God" or first cause is alien to the Buddhist philosophy of becoming—no beginning, no end, only eternal change, impermanence, everything coming into being dependent on everything else. Whatever occurs does so because of innumerable causes. If one grain of sand on a beach is moved, this affects the whole beach and ultimately the universe. Nothing comes from nothing.

Also, the meaning of the word "God" is as varied as our personal perceptions. We each imagine God according to what we need, what we are taught, or what we have experienced. The creator God can be seen as a father, a universal ruler, a vengeful despot, an immovable fate, a savior or a destroyer—whatever society needs at a particular time.

The supreme god of the Buddha's time was Brahma. Only priests knew him. Because of their knowledge, they mediated between the gods and humanity. Only priests could offer sacrifices donated by the people, and only they could interpret divine instructions. The priests were Brahmins, and one had to be born into that caste to be a Brahmin. Brahma—the notion of *ultimate Self* in India at that time—was in many respects similar to the Jewish-Christian-Islamic concept of God.

The idea of an ultimate Self and a personal soul was the main religious belief of the Buddha's time. The personal soul reincarnated again and again in different life forms and in different circumstances until it was so purified that it returned to or was united with its creator, the ultimate Self (God). The personal soul was considered to be the thinker of one's thoughts, the feeler of one's sensations, and the receiver of rewards and punishments for one's good or evil deeds. This Brahmin idea of the self is also the Western philosopher Descartes' idea of self—"I think, therefore I am." The desire of every believer in the Brahmin religion was to be united at last with the ultimate Self—united with God.

It was not the Buddha's custom to contradict the beliefs of those who came to question him. Instead, he used folktales, parables, metaphors and examples that would be intelligible to a particular person. His method of teaching was to encourage the questioner to do his or her *own investigative thinking*. And there are several instances in Buddhist texts where the Buddha did not answer certain questions—not because he didn't know the answer, but because at that time, the inquirer wasn't able to understand what was being said.

When it is misunderstood, the doctrine of *no self* fills the non-Buddhist with fear that if impermanence is true, then after the body dies there must be an annihilation of the self. Oblivion! Nothing! Out like an extinguished candle! Such fear is understandable without a correct view of the Buddha's teaching of no soul.

There is probably more mistranslation and misunderstanding about this one teaching of the Buddha on *self* and *soul* than the rest of his teachings put together! There are thousands of people who consider themselves Buddhists who do not understand this teaching.

As in the Buddha's time twenty-five hundred years ago, the soul is seen by most religious people today to be an entity apart from the physical body, eternal and not subject to change, given by God and taken back to God at the moment of death, or shortly thereafter. Sometimes the soul is spoken of as the breath of God—breathed into the body at birth and withdrawn at death. This soul is said to be the seat of the emotions, as when someone says they were "stirred to the depths of their soul." Sometimes the soul is seen as pure and the body is seen as foul. In this case, the body must be subdued in order to liberate the soul from its prison. There is also the belief that the pure soul can be corrupted by the impure body. This leads to belief in salvation and damnation—our soul can be saved or sent to everlasting torment, even though it is the gift or breath of God.

The soul is seen as the individual, the person. Taken further, the soul becomes the *real* I, an unchangeable core of personal being.

The Buddha, however, taught that there is no eternally unchangeable, concrete entity called the soul.

No Self? No Me?

WHEN A PERSON is told there is no such thing as an I, they hear that *they* do not exist, that there is no identity called John or

Ann, that what they see before them in the mirror does not exist. Without further investigation, no wonder they think their informant should be locked up quietly in an asylum!

For centuries before and after the Buddha, right up to this present moment, people have done violence to their body and mind in a desperate effort to negate the "I." For the Buddhist this is unnecessary and sadly misleading. There is no "I." And if something doesn't exist, it isn't possible to negate it. Even full enlightenment won't get rid of the "I." What Buddhism teaches is *not* the need to get rid of the "I," but to understand the nonexistence of such a phenomenon.

What is this "I" that so many seekers after truth in various religions try to understand? What is this "I" that seems to be our most precious possession? Whole libraries of philosophical works have been and will continue to be written about this "I," so important is the idea of "I" to us!

This very importance holds the answer to the question of what is the "I." The "I" is an *idea.* The "I" is merely a *label.* The "I" doesn't exist any more than the label on a jam jar is the jam itself. The jam can be said to exist because we can see it, touch it, taste it and smell it, but the jam is not the same as the label "jam."

"I" is a label we place on collections of material forms, sensations, perceptions, mental formations and moments of consciousness which themselves are constantly changing. Just what are we labeling? What is *"me"* at any given moment?

This "I", to which we desperately cling as eternally unchanging, is an impossibility, but the *idea* is useful as a label for the phenomenon, the person. Therefore, there *is* an I or self, but it is only a label for use in *conventional truth*—the truth by which we function in the world. *Ultimate truth*, however, shows us the nonexistence of any solid, concrete, inherently existing phenomenon that is *me*.

We are so accustomed to acting and reacting with labels that we seldom investigate what the label is really attempting to describe. We use mental and verbal shorthand most of the time to facilitate everyday human communication—conventional truth. But is it what we as individuals *really* think?

Buddhism teaches that existence is in a constant state of flux. Nothing remains the same for even the blink of an eye. A little investigation shows this to be true. Because of impermanence, nothing exists *inherently* or in isolation, created by itself. Whatever is at any moment depends on everything else that is at that moment and ever was anywhere. When we move a grain of sand, when a leaf falls, when we breathe, even when we think—we have made a change in the universe. Whatever we may think, what we refer to as the soul, the self, the I is also subject to change—it is a compound phenomenon.

Taking the mind to be the self is no better than taking the body to be the self. The mind or consciousness is subject to even more rapid change than the body. Every moment of thought is change and impermanence.

Let me repeat that the teaching of *no self* is not to be thought of as, "I have no self" (nihilism). This is as incorrect as the thought, "I have self" (eternalism). The skillful way to understand the teaching is objectively to investigate the matter for yourself. Nihilism would directly contradict the teaching of impermanence. This teaching is not of an end, but of *constant change*. After this moment comes another *different* moment. Our existence is a continual adventure. Even the Buddhist symbol of a wheel as the circle of existence is too static a symbol. All phenomena arise from conditions. Because we believe and live in a seemingly solid world, this fluidity is difficult to experience. But personal investigation and meditation will make it a real experience.

Nothing—nothing at all—remains the same for even less than a nanosecond. Nothing. Not a seed, not a blade of grass, not a flame, not the most beautiful object, not the strongest passion, not the sharpest sorrow, not our bodies, our ideas or even our opinions. We pay little notice to this fact in our everyday lives. But whether we are aware of it or not, everything is in a constant state of change. This includes mountains, gold bars and steel girders.

Most of our pain and suffering can be attributed to ignoring or denying impermanence. When we are in trouble, we feel that there is no way out, that misery will go on forever, that our pain will never soften. Sometimes we feel that even death won't release us from our suffering. Yet whatever our situation is, it is constantly changing—and sometimes for the better.

The other side of this picture is the expectation that what we *grasp* at is unchangeable. We don't see that our most prized possessions are dissolving before our eyes. When we become even faintly aware of this, we try to lay the blame on anything but the truth of impermanence. When friendships cool or lose their intensity, we suffer. We experience our business expanding and expect it to expand without altering—except to our own advantage. If we were able to accept *fully* the truth of impermanence, we'd realize that things are changing all the time. We'd realize that if we are aware and act skillfully, things may turn out better than at first seemed possible. As for what we want to remain unchanged, we'd realize this is impossible. We'd realize that all we really have is *now*, the given moment. We would appreciate the moment so much more. Our families, loves, friends, fellow beings and our own planet home would be precious to us. Our words and acts would be wise. Our personal aversions and squabbles would seem childish and futile. We'd see the energy we put into carrying burdens of unresolved guilt and resentment from the past as a waste. The realization—the *making real to our minds*—of the truth of impermanence would enlighten us and lessen the pain of suffering for ourselves and others.

So much suffering stems from ignorance!

We are ignorant of the fact that nothing exists *inherently* of itself. Again, that is not to say that nothing exists or that I can sit safely in the middle of traffic because passing cars don't really exist. It is only to say that no *thing* exists. Phenomena are dependently arising—causes are effects of other causes and other effects, *ad infinitum*. In the bargain, they don't exist in a particular state even for a nanosecond. If things can be said to exist at all, it is a momentary existence, almost too momentary to be called existence. We accept our *labels* as permanent things—car, house, person named Joan or Andy, the *status quo*, my idea of me. But our labels—"car," "house," "Joan," whatever I call "me," and so on—simply indicate a vast collection of ever changing phenomena. Last year's car is not today's car. Joan is not the girl I once knew. I am no longer what I was in the past—and the changes are much quicker than that.

Emptiness

THIS DOCTRINE OF no *inherent* existence of a self is also called the teaching on *emptiness*.

When I first became interested in Buddhism more than forty years ago, I couldn't grasp this teaching at all. I decided to put the question aside and come back to it later. Although I never consciously came back to it, as my Buddhist education advanced I must have learned something, because one day it occurred to me that I had imagined the Buddha's teaching on emptiness to be beyond my capability to understand. Because of this attitude I hadn't really listened or applied my mind to what I heard. On that day I suddenly gave the correct answer to a question put to me on the subject. I said these words: "Emptiness of *inherent* existence—nothing existing from its own side—dependent origination." I had understood. Everything—every event, every phenomenon coming into and going out of existence—depends on everything else, which depends on everything else in turn. This is a marvelous web of being.

No self means "empty of inherent existence." There is no self as we are accustomed to perceive it. No inherently existing, eternal person, personality, soul, spirit or whatever we like to call it.

The key word that is often missed is *inherently*. Our idea of self is of a solid entity, unconnected with anything else—an unchanging, inherently existing, permanent I residing in a changing body.

Someone says, "I am Joe (or Joan) Smith." We ask, "Who is J. Smith?" The person points to their chest, "*I* am J. Smith." Then we can begin to investigate.

"Is that torso to which you point J. Smith?"

"No."

"Is the hand with which you point J. Smith?"

"No."

"Are the legs on which that torso rests J. Smith?"

"No."

"Is the mouth that frames these replies J. Smith?"

We can carry on in this way until we have metaphorically shredded the flesh of J. Smith and drawn out the marrow of J. Smith's bones. A Zen master might give the person before him a whack with his stick and tell them to get out and come back when he or she had found J. Smith! The simple answer, of course, is that "J. Smith" is merely a label used for that particular, ever-changing, part-of-everything-else bundle of matter, sensations, perceptions, thoughts and moments of consciousness.

This process of investigation can be carried out on any object you care to name, although a teacher is recommended and even necessary for truly understanding this philosophy. No *thing* can be said to inherently exist, only collections of energies that are continually changing form and position. This is what Buddhism calls *emptiness*—modern scientific findings taught by the Buddha more than twenty-five hundred years ago.

"Interesting," you may say, "but how does this help me cope with *daily* suffering?" When all the esoteric teachings and cultural overtones are put aside, the teaching of the Buddha is based on his compassionate wish for us *to free ourselves* from daily suffering. How can this come about?

First, the teaching on emptiness shows us that karma is not some supernatural form of punishment and reward. It is straightforward and common sense. Our *actions* of body, speech and mind, dependent on all phenomena for their coming into existence, in turn have an effect on everything else. We can see this in our everyday lives. When one person in a family, group or team is in a particularly pleasant or bad mood, this mood occurs from many causes, and it has many effects. These effects ripple outward, sometimes with infinitesimal vibrations.

This is happening *all* the time, *everywhere*. It is the reason the world is as it is, or has become, at *any* moment. Each of us contributes skillfully or unskillfully. Each of us is partly responsible. Sometimes the effects of our actions are immediately apparent. Other times, we ourselves may never become consciously aware of them. We may be, and often are, giving help or causing trouble without realizing it.

This is a basic and important part of the Buddha's teachings. Without fully understanding this, we cannot proceed to the deeper teachings. Many people make the mistake of chasing after a quick road to enlightenment. I know that road only too well. It comes before one fully realizes—truly understands—that the path begins right here and now with ourselves. We need to take the time to understand and contemplate these simple truths. We can't put the top story on a building before we have laid a solid foundation. Of course, setting a solid foundation is hard work. It means transforming our own minds. But no one can *give* us enlightenment. Enlightenment is not a matter of having faith in or believing the Buddha's teachings. It's a matter of fully understanding them, and this is personal.

When a Buddhist calls this existence—our unenlightened condition—"mere illusion," this means simply that existence is not as we are *used to* viewing it. We view the world without *awareness* of the lack of inherent existence, without awareness of impermanence, and so we accept the way we are used to viewing things (not truly so) as reality. We live our lives accordingly, clinging to illusions as if trying to grasp a lover in a dream. We see things the way we *think* they are, or should be, and we act in error. We are like bulls in china shops in our dealings with existence. We think that lightning-quick reactions are always wise, but they are only wise when we are fully aware of the circumstances surrounding an event. We are so sure we know everything, yet we don't even know the thoughts and true feelings of the person sitting next to us, nor do we really understand our own.

Think, for example, of love or hate at first sight. The object of the emotion appears to us to be desirable or disgusting. The truth may be so, may not be so, may be the other way around, or may be somewhere in between, yet we are *sure* we are *absolutely* correct in our view of the situation. When what is desirable seems to change into something disgusting, we are devastated. Later, we are surprised when what we had thought of as disgusting turns out to be nothing of the sort. It was an *illusion.* This goes on with us all the time—day in, day out—confusion heaped on confusion. It creates broken friendships, parent–child rifts, romantic tragedies, unhappiness and suffering for everyone—just because we are reluctant to take into account as much as possible in a given situation before acting.

You might ask, of what use to us can knowledge of emptiness be? When phenomena are seen as unconnected and unchanging, we may make hasty, mistaken judgments. We think mountains are blue because from a distance they appear to be blue. We believe the person who did not reply to our greeting despises us. We turn discussions into arguments and wars because we see those whose ideas are different from ours as enemies. We seem incapable of accepting people as they are without putting our own labels on them—incapable of letting them be, of giving them the respect and space we hope to receive ourselves. We see everything as good or bad, right or wrong, and so on.

ULTIMATE AND CONVENTIONAL TRUTH

IT WILL HELP to look at things a little differently. There are for Buddhists (and physicists) two forms of truth. In Buddhism, these are called *conventional truth* and *ultimate truth*. We may be accustomed to the idea that truth is truth is truth, but the explanation of *two* truths is really quite simple and useful.

The Buddhist theory of emptiness—lack of *inherent* existence of all compound phenomena—is similar to the theory of relativity. It is existence as it is now being explained by physics. When we examine any thing minutely, right down to its neutrons and beyond, we find a vast emptiness. The "thing" examined doesn't exist as we are used to perceiving it. Put simply, this is *ultimate truth*, that everything is illusion (not truly as we are used to viewing it).

The second truth, *conventional truth*, is the truth with which we function in the world. We accept our sense-based perceptions as reality. Physicists who see ultimate truth through experiments and theories still drive easily to a "real" home in a "real" car after work. They use "real" instruments for investigation, write "real"

reports at a "real" desk—all of which they *know* to be "unreal"—
yet they are able to make use of things that exist *conventionally*.

A Buddhist aims to be aware of these two types of truth at all
times, never being aware of only one.

Now, it might seem that full awareness—realization of ultimate truth—would make normal life impossible. It would cause
all sorts of physical and mental difficulties. But on the contrary, it
can help us see situations more clearly and react more skillfully,
avoiding unpleasant or even dangerous retaliations or reactions.

Consider the teachings the Buddha gave to the people of the
kingdom of Kesaputta. These people were collectively known as
the Kalamas. They were wondering what to believe when every
believer in Brahma and every ascetic who came by insisted that
their truth was *the* truth. This was the Buddha's advice to them:

> Yes, Kalamas, it is proper that you have doubt, that you
> have perplexity, for a doubt has arisen in a matter which
> is doubtful. Now, look you Kalamas, do not be led by
> reports, or tradition, or hearsay. Be not led by the author-
> ity of religious texts, nor by mere logic or inference, nor
> by considering appearances, nor by the delight in specu-
> lative opinions, nor by seeming possibilities, nor by the
> idea: "this is our teacher." But, O Kalamas, when you
> know for yourselves that certain things are wholesome
> and good, then accept them and follow them.

The Buddha told his followers to examine even him so that his disciples could be sure about the teacher they followed and have no doubt about the teaching—doubt being a hindrance to enlightenment unless it's used as an investigative tool.

Buddhism can be of no real value to an individual unless one learns to be perfectly honest with oneself. Not to learn this leaves us simply going through the motions, conforming to our culture's customs or trying to accept another culture, even shaving our head and wearing robes in the belief that this will activate enlightenment.

Being honest with oneself about oneself is not so easy as it sounds. There are times when shame or regret cause such mental anguish it would be easier to scratch an open wound with a wire brush than to investigate the cause, to accept one's part in the responsibility, and then to *let it go*. Buddhist practices are wonderful therapy for this kind of troubled mind, and that is part of what Buddha was getting at. This is why he taught his followers to do as he did—to meditate.

FIVE

How Can I Learn to Meditate?

To BEGIN WITH, Buddhist meditation does not mean going into a trance. A person in a trance state isn't aware of what's going on around them. During Buddhist meditation, you become more, not less. aware of what is going on because your mind isn't distracted by chasing after every sensation and thought. Awareness becomes clearer and unattached or freed from clinging.

We tend to assume that we are fully aware. We don't realize how much we put between ourselves and real awareness. We are constantly seeking distraction with endless worry and with radio, television, newspapers, films and so on. We constantly want something to occupy our minds. We are used to being constantly entertained. We do anything—ANYTHING—rather than be aware of the way things really are and aware of what, out of it all, is important to us.

In order to become truly aware of what is going on, we need to stop following the mind's activities. Then, we will be able to act skillfully on behalf of ourselves and others.

Buddhist meditation is not achieved with pleasant sounds, comforting mental pictures, or putting one's problems aside for the time being. These popular forms of meditation are another way to not get down to the nitty-gritty of investigating the reality of our situations.

Well, if that is what Buddhist meditation is *not,* then what *is* it? The English word "meditation" was the nearest the early translators could come to the meaning of the Pali and Sanskrit word, *bhavana.* This word means "development" or "culture", as in mental development, mental culture, mental yoga. This is distinct from purely physical yoga, which the Buddha found didn't lead to enlightenment.

Meditation (*bhavana*) was practiced before the Buddha's time, but he considered the yogic mystic states gained through Brahmanic practices as mind-created, conditioned and not leading to full enlightenment. For the Buddhist, enlightenment is seeing things as they *really* are in the present moment. During his ascetic period, the Buddha had tried these other methods. Then he developed what is known as *insight meditation (vipassana* in Pali), which did lead to full enlightenment. This is true Buddhist mental culture.

Insight meditation deals with our bodies, feelings, sensations, the mind, and moral and intellectual subjects. In the process, Buddhist meditation develops mind control—control of one's *own* mind.

Why is control of one's mind so important? *Where the mind goes, the body tends to follow.* A controlled mind can be directed skillfully, while an uncontrolled mind chatters like a "drunken monkey" and its misperceptions lead to unskillful behavior and unnecessary suffering. A controlled mind can clearly absorb the overall picture. An uncontrolled mind is too full of narrow concerns to get more than momentary glimpses of what's really happening.

Buddhist meditation is useful for those who feel a need to learn how to see clearly what life is about and why events occur as they do. If you feel a need to live life a way that does less harm to yourself and others, you have the potential to gain much from Buddhist meditation.

In order to begin to meditate, it's important to meditate as regularly as possible. Whether your meditation session lasts ten minutes or an hour or more, a beginner gets the best results if meditation is done at a predetermined time. This small discipline of establishing a regular practice is the beginning of leading a more disciplined life. It will bring many benefits of mental and emotional stability.

The most productive times for meditation are early morning, noon and evening. An early morning session sets the tone for the day. A noon session calms the worries that have accumulated so far and provides a clearer view of difficulties. An evening session clears the mind to sort and solve the day's intake of impressions. It allows an untroubled sleep—not a bad return for one and a half, or even a half hour, of one's day. Practicing meditation will soon show the amazing ability of an undistracted mind to see daily problems clearly and in context, instead of seeing them unclearly or not at all when we are up to our necks in them.

It's advisable not to force yourself to do long periods of practice to the point where aversion to practice arises. Training the mind is like training an unruly animal. Work gradually until the mind begins to look forward to the meditation training sessions. You can increase your time in meditation at this point.

If you are an advanced meditator, the question of *where* to meditate is simply anywhere and everywhere. For the beginner, it's different. Choose the quietest room where you live, one in which you are least likely to be interrupted. Meditate on your cushion in this place regularly until you reach the point of not needing a special place. Clear a shelf, table or chest top. On a clean cover, place the following: your choice of a fresh flower, either in a vase or left to wither and be replaced (a reminder of impermanence), a candlestick and candle, a bowl of clear or perfumed water, and anything which you find engenders calmness or which can be a subject of your personal focus. An advantage of an "altar" like this is that, even when you are not involved in a session, the mere memory of this focal point will help to calm your mind by creating a mental association with the quiet of meditation.

Before your morning session, clean and arrange your altar. Arrange fresh flowers and offerings and light the candles. These actions in themselves are offerings of respect and gratitude for the Buddha and his teachings and offerings for the well-being of all sentient beings. (This preparation for meditation differs slightly according to the religious beliefs and practices of the meditator and individual preferences.)

The correct and best position for meditation (although not the only one) is cross-legged.

The spine should be straight without stiffness, head bent slightly forward, shoulders relaxed, arms bent, right hand palm-up on top of the left palm in the lap, arms a little away from your sides, thumbs touching. Eyes may be closed or half-open. If half-open, the gaze may be directed at a point in front of you along the line of the nose, or directed just below eye level, which is also a good height for a visual focal point. The lips should be relaxed—not pressed together and not sagging apart. The tongue should lightly touch the back of the upper teeth. Breathe through the nostrils to prevent the mouth from becoming dry.

Hands together with thumbs touching is a way of closing the energy circuits of the body. When first using this position, you may have fleeting muscle pains. Don't try to ignore your discomfort. Instead, direct the mind to the trouble spot and mentally investigate it in every aspect. Where exactly is the pain? How deep inside is it? What kind of pain is being experienced?

Eventually, discomfort will ease and the muscles will adapt, but fighting discomfort will cause only more tension.

The most basic meditation practice is "watching the breath." This requires you to be fully aware of the coming and going of the breath through the nostrils without consciously thinking about it. Although we may become aware of our rapid or deep breathing during physical exertion, we rarely are aware of the breath as it enters and leaves the body through the nostrils, of feeling the breath on the skin between our nostrils and upper lip. In meditation, practice concentrate effortlessly on this incoming and outgoing of the breath.

While watching the breath like this, sounds, sensations and flashes of thought may attract your attention. Let such phenomena enter and leave awareness without following or clinging to them. Awareness remains, but grasping does not occur. On becoming aware of distraction, bring your consciousness back to the sensation of the breath entering and leaving the nostrils.

There are many variations on *watching the breath* meditation, such as counting inhalations and exhalations up to ten over and over, or counting the breaths up to ten and then from ten to one. Regardless of which method you choose, the object of these exercises is to be *fully aware* of whatever you are doing.

With these apparently simple exercises, you are learning the concentration necessary for further progress. It is not possible to achieve successful mind control without first learning not to be distracted by the song of a bird, a voice, traffic noises, the scent of flowers or any of the sensory effects of everyday life. The highest meditation is a *learned* skill. When acquiring any skill, the most important part of the training is the basic part. No base, no progress. No foundation, no house.

The initial benefits of meditation are quickly achieved if you are confident and willing to persevere. Your health and daily relationships will improve with the calmness and serenity induced by the practices. You will become more aware of your actions of body, speech and mind in relation to others, and how this affects their reactions to you. This leads to greater harmony.

This concentration on actions and feelings is not designed to produce self-consciousness. Don't meditate with thoughts like, "I am breathing in, I am breathing out," and so on. Forget your self and lose yourself in breathing. Let it be not "my" breathing but *simply breathing*. This is how all great works are achieved. Having learned a craft, the artist, writer, musician or scientist simply does their craft without consciousness of self.

Once you have learned not to grasp at distractions, there are many subjects you can take for your basic meditation. Your own body is a suitable subject. Begin with the skin, with all its sensations of temperature and tactile experience. Then imaginatively investigate each organ of the body and its function. When the body has been thoroughly mentally dissected, imagine its emptiness of *inherent* existence. Be aware of it as a *connected* whole, with each part relying on others for its ability to function, and they on it. This exercise is one that is used in the search for what we call "I" or the soul.

Now investigate the mind. Observe how thoughts arise and go, but don't follow them. If a particular thought persists, often a psychological or daily life problem, take it as a meditation subject. Investigate it from all angles without emotional attachment. This requires the strictest honesty regarding yourself.

While investigating your mind, simply be aware of the state of the mind. Is it overpowered with hatred and thoughts of revenge? Is it full of compassion, clarity of understanding and contentment? You are not the judge or a critic deciding between right and wrong. The meditator is a *non*-attached observer, not emotionally involved, just watching how feelings arise, seeing them, and watching how they pass. Thoughts and feelings don't engender second thoughts and feelings about them. Don't worry about your worries!

At first, this meditation works best with guidance from a teacher. Once you acquire the technique, you can use it to gain insight into what is really happening so you can handle situations more skillfully. Here it's important to learn that we are responsible for our own actions and reactions. We should be able to see clearly that other people and circumstances do not *make us* happy, sad, angry or anything. We *choose* to react in a certain way based on our perceptions, emotions and conditioning.

Walking can be a form of meditation, too. In some Buddhist temples and monasteries, this is done single file with time kept by individual walkers striking small metal triangles or wooden drums. However it is done, the pace is slow and full attention is being given to the movements of the body, especially the feet. Hands are held at chest level, and the gaze is directed at the ground about three feet in front.

Watching the breath is the basic type of meditative practice. No matter where we are, whether we're in a palace or prison, we are breathing. The body with its functions and sensations is also always present, as is the mind. It follows that externals such as altars and images are merely for the purpose of concentrating the attention or bringing to mind further subjects for contemplation—or so it ought to be.

Whether of a religious, philosophical or ethical bent, a Buddhist has a wealth of meditation subjects to choose from. Anything and everything can be used as a subject in Buddhist meditation once you have gained the ability to concentrate your attention without effort.

The most edifying subject is *universal compassion.* I touched on this earlier as a way to work with hatred or aversion. In this meditation you imagine you are with three other persons. To your right stands the one you love the most. To your left stands the one you dislike, hate or fear the most. In front stands a stranger to whom you are indifferent. Imagine that all human beings have existed thousands of times previously as human beings, male and female, with different dispositions. Now, exchange the one you love the most for the one you hate the most, then for the one to whom you are indifferent. Do this for each in turn, on and on, remembering that each person at some time has been your loving mother or father, your enemy, or a person of complete indifference. (This is not an uncommon experience in everyday life. We don't need to believe in "many lives" to experience that a friend changes into an enemy, a stranger become very dear, or an enemy becomes a friend.) If having existed countless times is difficult to accept, contemplate that every sentient being is subject to suffering in *this* life. Use this contemplation to nurture compassion for all.

Another set of four well-known subjects for meditation is called the *Four Sublime States:*

1. Loving kindness—extending unlimited, universal love to all beings
2. Compassion for all suffering beings
3. Sympathetic joy in the success, welfare and happiness of others
4. Equanimity—being able to face whatever occurs with a calm, undisturbed mind

These four are aims of all practicing Buddhists, regardless of sect or culture.

Loving kindness, sympathetic joy, equanimity and universal compassion are not sentimental. You aren't expected to weep on the neck of the child molester or sadist. Simply recognize that

Buddha nature—the potential to be enlightened—exists in every sentient being, whether that potential is developed or not.

Universal compassion is an attitude of mind that recognizes the criminal as a fellow suffering sentient being. What you do to improve matters is another question, but your practice of compassion doesn't demand personal contact. Instead, it aims at always having real empathy and sympathy. Universal compassion won't cause you to neglect your own defense. However, whatever you do in defense will be done without anger.

Here are other subjects for meditation—qualities for us to develop. These are called the *Seven Factors of Enlightenment:*

1. Mindfulness—being aware and mindful of all activities of body, speech and mind
2. Investigation into our own religious, ethical and philosophical beliefs
3. Energy and determination to do this, to finish what one begins
4. Joy or the opposite of gloomy pessimism
5. Relaxation—not being stiff physically or mentally
6. Concentration
7. Equanimity—being able to face whatever occurs with a calm, undisturbed mind

If you are interested, try these practices for yourself. To practice Buddhist meditation doesn't mean you automatically become a

Buddhist. It is a matter of personal experience. Really, this is your business. How you live your life is your own responsibility.

Buddhist meditation is not a do-it-yourself subject. Initially, to learn to meditate requires a trusted teacher to set the would-be meditator on the right path.

There are teachers to be found at any Buddhist study center, and there are countless books on the subject that you can access. But let me express some words of caution. Don't take written words as concrete fact, absolute instruction or commandment. This would be to waste the Buddha's advice of thinking for yourself. What meditation achieves develops stage by stage. This will be experienced differently by each person. If an accomplished, advanced meditator described the experience, it wouldn't be the exact experience of anyone else. The only way to understand an experience is to experience it. Try meditation for yourself. It is nearly impossible to put personal experience into comprehensible words. Hoping for someone, even the Buddha, to give us enlightenment shows how far we still have to go. There is only so much guidance you can be given—or need. Once you are past the preliminary stages, you will be very capable of carrying on with only occasionally "touching base" with your teacher. A meditation teacher only offers guidelines, puts up signposts and draws maps. The most accomplished master can't do more. The recipe is not the cake, the instruction is not the experience, and the map is not the treasure chest.

Perhaps the most helpful place to begin is by asking yourself,

"Why do I want to learn to meditate? What do I expect to gain from the practice? What type of meditation am I looking for?"

These are very important, personal questions for the would-be meditator. You are on your way to meditating once you have answered these questions for yourself. Every journey begins with deciding on your direction and then taking the first step. You must answer these questions to your own honest satisfaction. If you have spent some time on them, you have begun to meditate already.

Now, go and buy a book on how to meditate. There is help everywhere you turn if you are really serious in your search to learn how to meditate. Now that you have come this far, you only need a little luck and a little more effort to start your own journey into Buddhism.

We practice meditation until we have developed a new way of seeing people and situations. This takes *practice*—like learning to sing or do anything else well. There is no quick fix. Whatever meditation practice you do, just do it. Have no expectations of rapid success. Don't hedge your participation with expectations. Meditate on the difference between reality and your expectations. Don't waste time blaming things and people for not being what you expected them to be. Everything that happens is a chance to learn something more than you may know, or think you know. Meditation is not easy, but it's certainly not impossible. Simply start with an open mind. Do it. Begin now.

There are thousands—perhaps even hundreds of thousands— of people in the world trying to meditate. They try in temples, monasteries and caves, under trees and in quiet corners of their houses. They try on cliff tops and mountains. They try in groups and solitude.

There are countless books to be had on the subject and many competent teachers to be found, yet still people say, "I can't meditate. I've tried and tried. Show me how to meditate."

Something is wrong somewhere. Are the places where we seek to meditate the wrong places? Are the books and teachers wrong? If the instruction is clear and the student is mentally able to absorb it, surely *trying* to meditate should bring about the desired result? Is this some kind of weird joke? Why can't someone just tell me plainly how to go about trying to meditate?

I don't profess to actually teach anything, but my advice is that if you are *trying* to meditate then stop immediately. It is a waste of effort. It obviously isn't working, so give it up. You'll feel much better, and the relief will be bliss. What do you have to lose but tension?

You did all your preliminary practices and then tried, very hard, to meditate. Nothing happened. No visions, no peace of mind. Instead all the thoughts you tried to get rid of welled up and distracted you. The more you tried to push them away, the stronger they became. These thoughts had nothing to do with meditation, or so you think—they were exactly what meditation was supposed to free you from!

Perhaps pleasant thoughts distract you: quiet beaches, snowy mountain peaks, soft floating clouds. Now you can drift away from dull or worrying everyday life. Ah, that is better. Then the meditation tape you were listening to comes to an end and you know in your heart that you have not been meditating. How do you know this? Because your mind is not clearer now than when you started trying to meditate. Nothing is solved or resolved or cleared up. Yes, you may feel refreshed but a short nap would have done the same with better results.

My advice to anyone who is still struggling to meditate is this—give it up. Stop *trying* to meditate. It won't work.

Now, go back to the instructions you received. Follow *these*.

Prepare yourself for meditation. Note that I did not say prepare yourself *to meditate*. Meditation is not something you *do*. It is a mental state. What occurs in that state is called meditation. The quickest way to achieve that state is to stop *trying* to meditate. We have all experienced not being able to recall a memory—a name, a date, where we left the car keys or the time of an appointment. Yet within minutes of stopping trying to recall the information sought—there it is!

Remember how your teacher or that book on meditation gave you advice regarding your jumbled thoughts. *Do not try to stop them.* You can't! Thinking is a natural organic activity of the brain. Remember the simple advice to let the thoughts rise as they will, like bubbles in a glass of champagne. Some thoughts will be pleasant, some thoughts will be neutral, and some thoughts you would rather didn't rise at all.

As you sit there on your cushion have no goal, no expectations.

You are not trying to reach a certain level or state. You are simply watching your mind churning out thoughts. This is where you stop *trying* to meditate. Let the thoughts rise as they will, without plot or plan, and don't follow them emotionally, one way or another. Don't react, no matter what the thoughts are. This way you develop equanimity toward your own psychological makeup. And as you come to understand yourself through the practice of meditation, you will understand a great deal about existence.

There is no way anyone can learn to meditate for you. The paradox is that you must stop *trying* to do it. Just do it. This is a long, hard journey that each of us must make alone. You will know when it is done. This is the price we pay for our unique individuality. We can help each other along the way, but that is all.

Can you do it? Can you stop clinging to some goal, some idea of meditation as a place to get to? Meditation will come to you when you allow your thoughts to rise, without plot or plan, without you pursuing those thoughts with reaction or emotion.

In short, can you stop *trying* to meditate?

SIX

YOUR QUESTIONS ABOUT
BUDDHISM ANSWERED

IS IT POSSIBLE TO GAIN ENLIGHTENMENT LIKE THE BUDDHA?

DID THE BUDDHA *know all?* Did the Buddha know every detail of everything that had ever happened, was happening or would ever happen in the future, like a Jewish/Christian Jehovah? I don't think so.

When we say that a mechanic *knows all* about cars, do we mean that the mechanic knows a minute grain of floating dust has entered the fuel line and is intermittently blocking the flow of gas? I don't think so. Does the executive who *knows all* about how a company runs know that on a certain day a certain event will occur and throw someone off balance who will in turn send out a carelessly worded memo that will cause an uproar in a certain department where a certain person with emotional problems will throw a kink in the works? I don't think so.

At the moment of enlightenment was the Buddha suddenly aware of even the smallest, most mundane detail in the individual life of every sentient being? Was he aware of every event that would occur and its consequences? Every word that would ever be spoken or written and the effects these would have on every being? Was he suddenly aware of all the suffering to strike each individual—past, present and future—and the fate of every other sentient being? I don't think so.

What the Buddha and the mechanic and the executive all know is *how things work*. The wisdom of the Buddha lies in understanding the general principles of how things work. Can we acquire this type of omniscience? Can we learn *the general principles* of our existence? I *do* think so. In fact, I am sure of it. Buddha achieved this kind of omniscience and left us the instructions and signposts to make it possible. But it won't happen unless we put the teachings to full use. Like a musician, it requires that we practice, practice, practice. To *practice* does not mean doing the same thing over and over again. It means learning thoroughly and then going on.

Many religions have a deity who is the son of that religion's god. This theme has been repeated as long as humans have been practicing religion. If the Buddha were in this category, would it help in any way to learn to do as he taught? I don't think so, do you?

We need to look at what the Buddha taught from our own standpoint, not from traditional beliefs of long ago. Some of us need a teacher who has experienced what we must face in life. We need a teacher who made use of faculties that we possess, so that we have the chance to achieve what another human being has achieved. Then we can aim to achieve the humanly possible with every hope of success, can't we? I think so.

DOES BUDDHISM HAVE A PLACE IN EVERYDAY LIFE?

EVERYDAY LIFE IN the West does not differ fundamentally from everyday life anywhere else. All forms of life desire happiness and freedom from suffering. So, does Buddhism have a place in everyday life? The answer is no.

Why would I say that? I say it because Buddhism is not something to be tacked onto our everyday lives, like going to church on Sundays. Buddhism is itself a way of life that can give us happiness. It isn't like an aspirin that relieves our headaches for a while. Buddhism offers a way to find the causes of suffering and eliminate them.

In the West, we suffer in many ways. Whenever we want something and can't have it, or we lose it, or we fear losing it, *that* is suffering. Whatever we grasp at—freedom from hunger, the end of pain, youth, unchanging love, fame, wealth, praise or physical perfection—it is subject to impermanence. It doesn't matter whether we come from Asia, Europe, the Americas, Australia, Africa or anywhere else, everything is subject to impermanence.

Maybe, we in the West will gain more from Buddhism than those in Buddhism's traditional home because Westerners really have to work at Buddhism. We are subject to so much social pressure to appear affluent and progressive, and this can be at odds with Buddhist teachings.

It is really difficult to get out of the rat race we are in, and we *are* in it, like it or not. For some of us, the rat race has become addictive. The effort to keep up with and surpass others keeps a high level of adrenalin in our systems. It makes us feel vital. "Wow! I am a livewire!" we believe. When we stop for a while, our level of adrenalin drops and we feel lost. Now we suffer from boredom and feeling "out of it" or "over the hill."

We cannot reverse our Western technological progress. We cannot totally ignore technological advances—and we don't need to. We only need to adapt to the situation, see clearly what is what, understand ourselves, and understand why we do what we do.

Whatever our lifestyle, background or culture we all have very much the same personal problems. Wealth doesn't change this. The only way to eliminate these problems is to understand and eliminate their cause.

It isn't important whether the Buddha first outlined these teachings. What is important is that the teaching makes sense— it works. We shouldn't believe a word of the Buddhist teachings until we've thought deeply about them, meditated on them and then tried them out for ourselves. This certainly will do no harm.

Buddhism as a subject isn't easy, but nothing worth attaining is easy. The Buddha's teaching isn't static. It expands with our growth and understanding of it. One of the difficulties in our study is to separate the Buddha's philosophy from the cultural accretions that surround it after twenty-five hundred years of the teachings migrating from country to country. As the Dalai Lama advises, we should adapt these teachings to our own culture—not alter but adapt—without taking on cultural beliefs and practices that aren't our own. Remember, Buddhism is a way of life.

Why Do Buddhist Teachings Seem So Simple?

FOR MY FIRST six-week meditation retreat, my teacher gave me a small book and instructed me on how to use it. This retreat was going to be silent, with meals delivered to my door. I had decided I would walk daily in the grounds of the retreat property for exercise. Now that I had a book from my teacher and plenty of candles, I was quite, quite ready to meditate on the Buddhist teachings.

Then I looked at the book my teacher told me to use. I was indignant. This was kids' stuff! Kindergarten! Didn't he know I was not exactly new to the teachings? Maybe he didn't. I thought immediately that I would take the book back to him and tell him that I was more advanced than he seemed to realize. He would immediately understand that I was capable of taking in more profound teachings than the ones offered in this book. I certainly hadn't come halfway around the world and experienced so much discomfort and difficulty traveling in foreign countries to be mistaken for a mere beginner. I would go to him immediately.

But would I? What would I say to him? Was my retreat to be over before it had properly begun?

The long and the short of it was that I didn't go to my teacher—not for six weeks. In the meantime, using the little book as I had been instructed, I found it was a treasure, the value of which increased with each reading.

What were the instructions given to me by my meditation teacher? I dislike the thought of saying these instructions, knowing that people may dismiss them because they are "too obvious" or "simply common sense." Well, of course, they are obvious and common sense. That is Buddhism! Nevertheless, I offer to you what he told me so you can make use of it.

My teacher told me to read a small amount of the book and then meditate on its meaning. (I know now any book of the Buddha's teaching would have done equally well.) First of all, I had to spend a specified time to quiet my mind and clear it of distractions. Then I was to read and analyze thoroughly what I had read. Next I was to let it all go and meditate in a non-thought way, so that my deeper mind could get on with sorting it all out. Moreover, I couldn't go on until I was sure I had understood each section. Finally, and most important of all, I was not to believe—or fool myself that I believed—anything that didn't make sense to my mind.

It's nearly eighteen years since that retreat, and I have used this same method over and over again. It always works. I recommend it!

If you can apply this method to the teachings of the Four Noble Truths one by one, it will eventually lead to an *Alice Through the Looking Glass* experience in which everything you understand, know and experience is different yet the same, seen from quite another angle.

Perhaps the simple repetition of a text may lead to something becoming real to you. Other people may need to mull over and over a teaching before it finally sinks in. Finding the way that suits us personally, and finding a teacher with whom we have rapport, isn't easy. But is anything valuable ever easy? Perhaps we should begin applying *right effort* from the Eightfold Path. It's worth trying for a happier life, isn't it?

How Can I Find Serenity?

MOST OF US find it difficult to believe that it isn't what happens to us in life that's important, but how we choose to react to it.

Give the matter a few minutes of thought. When something irritates you, and you lose your temper over it, does that make it any better? Does it solve the problem? When you suffer a loss and withdraw from others, does your isolation really make your pain easier to bear? Both joy and pain need to be shared.

The way we react to events is of huge importance. If someone or something is irritating us or causing us physical or emotional pain, we can react in different ways. Often the way we react is dependent on our personality and past conditioning, especially the conditioning of early life in a family.

The Buddhist way is first to distance ourselves from what's causing us trouble. If we can't distance ourselves physically, we can do so mentally. This gives space in which to study the cause of our distress. Don't study anyone else. Don't study the event or person you see as the cause of your problem. Study your *own* reactions and discover why *you* react as you do. Is it a wounded ego? An unquiet conscience? Anger at what you see as betrayal of some kind? Look within, at your own part in your distress. In spite of popular belief, no one else can make you happy or sad, angry or serene. You are responsible for your own reaction to events.

If you feel someone has been unfair or unpleasant, remember that person is a suffering being like all of us. Don't add to their suffering or your own with a reaction that adds fuel to the flames. It isn't a matter of backing down or giving in. This is common sense. If you react to a situation with strong emotion, you're acting with a clouded mind. In this state, you can't act wisely in anyone's interest, your own or others.

If we consider a situation for a moment and meditate on it, it becomes clear that no one is to blame for our reactions but ourselves. We can control our emotions if we take the trouble to do what Buddhism teaches us. We can ask ourselves: Why am I so sad? Why am I so angry? What part am I playing in this? Is there anything I can do to make it better? Am I acting based on past actions?

If the last question is answered yes, see if there is anything that can be done to remedy the situation. If there's nothing to be done, then put the matter behind you. While regret is appropriate when we've been in the wrong, once we've done what we can to remedy things, guilt only clouds the mind. Guilt makes us seek someone to blame in order to rid ourselves of our own suffering; it corrodes sincere regret.

Yes, it is very, very hard to be absolutely honest with oneself, but it is the only path to true serenity. The prescription to cure our distress is mind control—control of our own mind. We can do this if we really want to. It is worth a try at least!

How Can I Feel More Secure and Less Fearful?

WE HUMAN BEINGS like to see ourselves as lords of creation. Don't most religions teach that we are made in the image of a supreme creator? We're told we rule over the planet earth. Surrounded by myriad life forms we believe that we are the most intelligent, the most evolutionarily developed and the only species of real importance. Therefore, we are entitled to subdue, conquer, enslave, use, improve or destroy the rest of the species and the earth's resources as we wish.

If this is true, why are we afraid? There is no doubt we feel fear. What do we have to fear? It's generally true that we fear *everything*. Why do we need a god to control the threatening chaos? Fear is the reason. We need a god to be in control of our lives, because we fear not being in control as strongly as we profess to be. We fear what we don't understand.

The basis of fear is insecurity. But if we analyze and meditate we see there is ultimately no such thing as lasting, hard-and-fast security for anyone, anywhere. What we fear *for* doesn't exist.

Truly knowing that our fears are groundless because everything is transient and impermanent leads to freedom from fear. Once we are free from fearing threats to our nonexistent security, we can appreciate what we have more deeply. Everything can be held more gently rather than tightly grasped. We can enjoy what we have as long as we have it. And when it goes, then someone else will have it for a while.

Why is there no lasting security? I suppose the reason lies in our idea of security. Most people call security the *status quo*. We want everything to remain as it is—at a point that we might consider to be perfection. For some people this point is one thing, for others it is something else.

Consider this: Is the blossom perfection, or is the ripe fruit ready for eating perfection?

Absolute security is unchanging perfection change, and this wish can never be granted. This prayer can never be heard, for the simple reason that nothing in existence remains the same for a nanosecond. Change is constant. Impermanence is true of everything, mental as well as physical phenomena. There is nothing to cling to, and no one to cling. If it weren't for the labels we use, there would be nothing graspable. Think about it. You don't need to go into a trance to contact emptiness. You are in it and part of it, like it or not—you and everything else.

When this emptiness, this impermanence, this nonexistence of security is understood, life is less distressing. Of course, delightful situations will change—and so will unpleasant ones. Loves will change—and so will hatreds. Change isn't necessarily negative. Negatives become positives, and vice versa. There is literally no thing to fear. Pain is subject to change. Even death is not sudden but a condition of gradual change—even when it appears to be instantaneous.

This Buddha Wisdom is as plain as dirt. A little meditation and consideration of what I'm saying will bring a clearer idea of what life is all about.

Why Are Consequences So Important in Buddhism?

BUDDHIST PHILOSOPHY TEACHES us to be aware. This doesn't mean we have to stuff our minds with every sight, sound, smell or sensation we can fit in. It means to be aware of what we are doing, the context in which we are doing it, why we are doing it, and its possible consequences.

The Buddhist teaching on awareness of consequences is the teaching of *dependent-arising*, the interconnectedness of everything. Nothing exists inherently. Nothing exists on its own. Everything at all times is changing into something else. It only requires a clear and open mind and a little meditation to show us that this is true.

For example, a blossom becomes a fruit or seeds, the seeds become sprouts, the sprouts become plants, and the plants produce flowers, which become seeds, and so on. The second flowering of the blossom isn't a replica of the first flowering because the circumstances for its production have changed according to other circumstances—different weather, different soil content, different growing position, and so on.

We ourselves aren't immune to constant change by any means. Our thoughts and opinions are constantly changing, as are those of everyone else. The consequences of our actions, our attitudes and our thoughts are as unavoidable as the first vibration that begins an avalanche on a snow covered mountain, the drop of water that results in a mudslide or the grain of sand that begins the movement of a sand dune.

Once we become fully aware of the significance of such matters in our personal lives, we become much more careful of how we act and think about other sentient beings, especially those with whom we have close contact, whether they are in our family, our workplace, shop attendants, fundraisers, or the opposition party in an election. Don't laugh. Who knows what type of effect one word has on another person's life, or what types of fears in another person our harsh words might be adding to? Small things can have devastating consequences, especially for people already staggering under difficulties we can't imagine.

Keep in mind that nothing begins from nothing. The angry words you receive for some minor matter don't begin with you. They are the consequence of something else in the experience of the speaker. No one escapes suffering—no one. If you are cultivating universal compassion inwardly, it will communicate to those in your orbit. Offer no egoistic defense, and the attack will have no target.

None of this is easy, but I know from my own experience that it works. Only meditation and practice will convince you of this. Although it's not easy, why not try it for a while and see for yourself?

How Can I Change My Attitudes that Cause Suffering?

IT IS FINE to understand greed, hatred and ignorance and to recognize them in oneself and others—but what can we do to overcome them? This is where we need guidance. These three have become almost second nature to us. We may even think we enjoy our passion, aggression and ignorance. The thought of breaking these habits may make the whole thing seem just too hard to be worth trying, another cause of more suffering, which is just what we are trying to avoid.

Well, as Buddhists we don't waste precious time trying to push greed, hatred and ignorance out of our minds. Instead we gently transform these attitudes, and the teachings show us how to do this. If we have learned correctly, the transformation is surprisingly easy. It becomes a matter of seeing things for what they really are and then relaxing the attitude that sees them as sources of lasting satisfaction.

Of course, there is a starting point to transformation, which is this: Do we really want to behave more skillfully? Do we really want to end our suffering? Do we really want to find peace of mind and happiness? Do we want it with all our being?

If we don't, then the teaching will be of no use to us. It is our choice entirely. The teachings can't cure us of our ignorance and suffering; they can only point the way. We have to make the journey ourselves. There is no savior to lean on, no one to bend down out of heaven and pull us into the pure lands by our hair, no ritual that can transform us miraculously. But there's no need to feel we are lost and lonely travelers because there is help along the way and many companions on the same path.

Regarding hatred, how can we begin to transform hatred into its opposite—wise, loving compassion?

The first thing to realize is that the hatred we are going to transform is inside ourselves—it is internal, not external. There is no force with which we can eliminate another's delusions until we understand and eliminate our own. It only causes further hatred when we try.

The Buddha taught that every being is only seeking happiness and comfort. That is what makes us do what we do. This is what makes any organism do what it does. Sometimes we look for mental or emotional comfort. Sometimes we simply want basic physical comfort. This search for physical and mental comfort—the search for happiness, avoiding discomfort and unhappiness—is the basis of survival. We love what makes us comfortable, and we hate what appears to threaten our comfort.

If we believe in reincarnation, it follows that any person, including our enemy, has at some time been our loving mother. They cherished and cared for us after bearing us in discomfort and pain. They fed and protected us and taught us the things we needed to know. When hate rises in us at the sight or thought of an enemy, using the concept of reincarnation we can put aside the negative attitude and remember the kindness done to us in the past.

If we don't believe in reincarnation, simply remember that everyone suffers, everyone knows loss and grief, and everyone feels threatened. See this in your enemy's face. It will help allay your mind.

Or if the Buddhist teaching that every person has been your mother doesn't touch you, remember that even if your mother abandoned you at birth, she still gave you the most precious of all gifts—the gift of a human birth. No matter what happened to you, you are here today, physically able to understand what I am saying, able to take the first steps out of confusion and free yourself from the acid of greed, hatred and ignorance. Truly, we owe our mothers an immeasurable debt.

If you try to see a situation from your enemy's point of view and ask yourself why you see them as an enemy, your hatred will subside. You will feel compassion for their present and future sufferings. This feeling will arise if you are very honest with yourself and stop blaming the enemy for your suffering mind. Having compassion for our enemy doesn't mean we need to have contact with them.

Often the kindest thing we can do is to keep away unless the time comes when they need our help. Then we should give that help without fear or anger.

In the case where you see yourself as your own worst enemy, don't be filled with self-hatred, but set about your own personal transformation with compassion. Train your thoughts as you would train a child or a fine animal—firmly, but with love.

Regarding greed, how on earth are we going to transform this attitude? If we substitute some other negative habit for the one we are trying to break, we'll be no further ahead—still unhappy and suffering. Greed and grasping will still be there.

In Buddhism, we renounce striving after illusion. There is nothing that doesn't eventually end in suffering if we expect it not to change. We will suffer because we cling to it. With the guidance of the Buddha's teaching we gradually lose our attachment to our personal gratifications and feel no pain in the loss of that attachment. It's not a loss, but a gaining of serenity. The law of impermanence guarantees that whatever we think will give us everlasting happiness will change from moment to moment. As we change ourselves. So how can we expect happiness to last? If we don't accept this truth, we're bound to suffer. Happiness is a state of mind, not the possession of something or someone. The teaching tells us to do what needs to be done with a good motive and without craving and attachment. In this way, greed is eliminated.

Really, transforming greed isn't a matter of giving up pleasant things but of enjoying them more! Take a simple example. Two friends at a party are each offered a slice of delicious cake. They accept. One of them gobbles his cake down as fast as he can, worried that someone will take it from him, or hoping to get another slice before the cake is completely given away. He watches suspiciously to see if his friend's slice is bigger or better and plots how to get some of it. He finishes his cake quickly, doesn't taste it, and suffers indigestion as well as the mental suffering of greed.

His friend takes his cake gratefully, aware of all the beings responsible for its existence, wishes all beings could share it with him, and enjoys everything about the cake—its taste, texture, smell and look. He eats it slowly and decently. He isn't giving up the cake—he is giving up the greed and attachment.

Finally regarding ignorance, what is the antidote to ignorance? Obviously it is *knowledge*, but knowledge about what?

Wisdom knowledge is the ability to see through illusion. By studying the Buddha's teaching and meditating on it, we come to understand what these illusions are. This is Buddha wisdom.

To see clearly through illusion requires a correct understanding of impermanence. Take memories, for example. Look back on your life and see it like a film. "This was this, and that was that. I did this, and they did that." Now, have you ever met someone who knew you then and asked them to tell their version of past events? It is a different story altogether. You have mixed fact with fantasy and dreams, and so has the other person. What is the truth of the matter? How could you or any confused person really know?

To think we see clearly is a delusion. We are what our heredity, environment and conditioning by family and society make us. From that position we create a view of existence—our view only.

We see things as good or bad, safe or dangerous, kind or cruel according to our own conditioning. We never let our minds reflect phenomena as they really are—clean, clear and undistorted by our concepts. We are aware only of what is filtered through our five senses and misconceptions. We proudly say, "I know what's going on," but do we?

We see ourselves as independently existing persons, surrounded by other people and things quite separate from ourselves. We think we manipulate people, objects and nature to our own or others' benefit or destruction. We fail to see that nothing and no one exists in isolation, owing nothing to anything or anyone else. We fail to see that no thing exists independently, inherently, of itself. Down to the minutest energy everything is interdependent and interconnected with everything else. All things, all phenomena, are empty—not nonexistent, but empty of inherent existence. All things are impermanent. Nothing exists inherently, on its own, without connection to other things.

In the Buddha's teachings, there are many new ways of viewing existence. They all point to one goal—*ultimate truth,* seeing things as they are. The Buddha also taught another truth—*conventional truth,* the truth by which we live in the world. A speeding car is a speeding car. If I stand in front of it, it will knock me down. This is conventional truth. The ultimate truth is that there is no such thing as a car. That's only a label we use to designate a certain combination of wheels, body and motor. These in turn are only labels for combinations of other things.

When we speak of "I" or "self," it is the same—a label for a combination of body-mind that also exists *non-inherently* and is subject to impermanence. This doesn't mean that the "self" or "I" will someday change. Certainly, the "Self" or "I" is changing every moment. Both truths are truths. Realizing these two truths together—conventional and ultimate—transforms ignorance into wisdom knowledge.

Why Is Generosity So Important in Buddhism?

WHAT DID THE Buddha mean by generosity? Is it of any benefit to others for me to practice generosity? Is it of any benefit to me? Does it make sense for me to aspire to it? After all, I'm no altruistic saint.

Generosity is not simply physically giving what we have to others we think are less fortunate than ourselves. Generosity can be seen in another light. True generosity comes from the heart. It is a state of mind. If we have absolutely nothing that we can give, we can still practice *generosity of mind*.

We can think mean, suspicious thoughts about others—sharply criticizing their ways, actions and speech, seeing the worst side of anything, belittling their efforts and intentions. Or we can ask ourselves the following questions:

Is it true?
Is it kind?
Is it necessary?

Simply because something is true there's no need to say it. Even if we consider it necessary to say it, is our motive pure? What are some of the possible consequences of saying it? Will it help anyone? Would it help or hurt the hearer or speaker? Again, what is our motive? Is it really necessary? If it *is* necessary, then we need to go through the list of whether it is true, kind and necessary and then check that our motive is pure.

The benefits are knowing that we are doing our best, in a way that seems to us the most generous, and knowing we haven't caused unnecessary pain to others.

Will Buddhism Help Me Get What I Want Out of Life?

WHAT EXACTLY DO you want? What would bring you real happiness? What would calm the lack of contentment that haunts you? If you think you know what you want, write it down as clearly and concisely as you can. Then refine what you have written down, so it is clear to you what will make you happy and satisfied forever, or for your whole life at least.

This isn't as easy as it sounds. Few people really know what they want. Most of us think we do but we haven't tried to express it clearly. And most of us either want everything or we want what we have no chance of possessing.

If we do not know what we want, how do we think we are going to get it? What do we do if it's unattainable? What do we do if it belongs to someone else? Is the answer not to want anything? Should we sit by the road with a dish in front of us and let the universe supply our needs? It's more likely the next truck will take care of all our needs by wiping us off the road. If we are not sure what we want, how do we think we will recognize it if it hits us in the face? It could appear before us, ready to be taken, and we wouldn't even know it was there.

There is a simple answer to the dilemma of how to get what you want. The answer is this: know what it is you want. Once you have defined the "want," you will be able to concentrate on it. As you do, you'll discard what doesn't work toward your goal, and you'll recognize everything that can be of aid to you. After a short while, it will seem like everything in your life is guiding you along the path to your heart's desire.

Then, if you understand the teachings of impermanence, dependent-arising and no self, you *will* be happy and blessed.

Of course, there's another way to get what you want and be happy but it is too simple to bother with. I hesitate to say it. If I told you this other way, you'd probably laugh and maybe even toss this book away. Well, all right, just for fun, I'll tell you. It is this—want what you get. Too easy and too simple, isn't it? Very well, go for the other one, but check your motives first.

*H*ow Does a Buddhist Cope with Loss and Grief?

PEOPLE HANDLE GRIEF and loss in their own way. There is no formula for making it easier. Loss can result from moving one's home. The loss of habits and home may be made more painful by the cause of the move. The new home may be a dream come true for the parents but not for the children, or vice versa. This loss can be worse for an elderly person who has to leave a home that holds so many memories. "But you'll have a lovely new room and company," a family member says. But what will become of their beloved pet or other treasures?

Loss of a loved person tears away a piece of the fabric of our lives. There is no such thing as quick mending for this type of loss. For how long do we feel that presence? Hear our name called? See the loved one in the face of a stranger? Grief is part of the lack of lasting satisfaction in existence. Grief is suffering.

The teaching that most helps Buddhists understand and accept the misfortunes of existence is the teaching of impermanence. Joy, youth, beauty and all the things we crave and cling to are constantly changing—and our misfortunes, sorrows and insurmountable problems are changing also. An understanding of impermanence offers a lifeline to keep us afloat as time does its healing work. Impermanence pertains to everything, even our grief.

The way to make this teaching work for you is through meditation on the impermanence and interconnection of all things. You will discover that the loss didn't happen *to* you at all; it happened because of everything else that has happened and is happening.

No matter how we try to deny grief, it will come out in some way, at some time, and cause more distress than it would have initially. It is better not to deny grief. There are healing properties in it.

Do You Have to Give Up Everything to Be a Buddhist?

BUDDHISM ISN'T DOOM and gloom. As Buddhists, we aren't expected to give up everything pleasant in life and cry about the mistakes we made in past lives—mistakes we can't even recall. We aren't expected to shut our eyes to what's beautiful. We aren't expected to sit cross-legged under a tree contemplating our navels. We don't believe that we can walk in front of speeding cars because cars don't exist. Buddhists enjoy chocolate, music and fun. Buddhists fall in and out of love like everyone else.

So What Is Different about Buddhists?

THE DIFFERENCE LIES where it can't easily be seen—in the mind. Buddhist teachings change the way we see and react to things. Buddhists try to understand emptiness—that everything is *empty of inherent existence*. We don't say *nothing* exists. What we say— what the Buddha said—is that no *thing* exists. Everything is connected and interdependent and grows out of what went before.

Buddhists do go on and on about impermanence. This is an important, yet such a simple teaching. Nothing lasts. Oh, misery! Everything is falling apart! Woe is me! My love affair won't last! My children won't always be sweet little babies! My house will eventually fall down—and so will I! These are events we don't want to think about, but are they so awful? Isn't it the natural way all things go? Everything is impermanent: joys, pleasures and also sufferings and miseries. Imagine if peaches remained peaches, eternally unchanged. We'd never be able to eat a peach, because eating it would change it. We would never see a peach tree blossoming.

Ignorance is another thing Buddhists go on about. We don't like to think of ourselves as ignorant, but Buddhism teaches that unless we are enlightened, we are ignorant about the way things are, ignorant of the way we contribute to most of our own problems, and ignorant of how we sow the seeds of our own future.

Every sentient being that's born suffers unhappiness in some form until the ultimate suffering of death. It is important to realize that this is really so. It takes thought and meditation to fully accept it. But there's no need for a long face! Once we clearly see this is true, we can drop the gloom and address why we personally suffer so much unhappiness.

The Buddha tells us that the cause of our own unhappiness is craving and clinging. We want, want and want. We want it now, and we want it to last forever. But nothing lasts and no thing exists, so we keep wanting something that we can't see for what it is, and we want what we think to last forever. No wonder we suffer.

Yet, even in the depths of this unhappiness we can cheer up because it doesn't have to be like this. There's a way out of mental suffering, a way to stop piling up unhappiness for ourselves and others. Although the Buddha taught for over forty years—I think sometimes he must have felt weary trying to drum sense into thick heads like mine—he said that the most important attribute we can aspire to is *compassion.* The compassion the Buddha taught is an attitude that wants all sentient beings to be free from suffering.

Compassion coupled with wisdom sees what needs to be done and does it. Buddhists endeavor to reach enlightenment as quickly as possible because then they will know how best to help all sentient beings. So if you see people apparently enjoying a nice "do nothing" snooze in Buddhist meditation they are really doing their utmost to be of use to all sentient beings. They may be meditating on a proposed form of action in order to do as good a job as possible. In any case, they are doing no harm.

There are many things we discover in Buddhist practice that can't be passed on to others, simply because each of us has to experience these things for ourselves. There is no point in words alone. We have to practice controlling the activities of our own mind until certain realizations come to us. Then we can laugh at the funny side of our ideas. For example, if you accept the idea of rebirth you can take it in one of two ways. You can moan, "Oh dear, I'll have to come back again and suffer some more," or you can smile at the thought of getting another chance.

Buddhists don't give up the pleasant things in life in order to overcome unhappiness. All we need to do is to give up our craving and clinging with an understanding of impermanence. Enjoy your love affair as precious because it will change. Enjoy your children and accept that they will change and grow up. Make your home comfortable while you live in it. Enjoy your own life every moment. Having accepted that nothing gives lasting satisfaction, having given up clinging, you will appreciate everything more. Change won't cause you suffering. One of the Buddha's teachings was simply to control your mind, and do no harm. Not bad advice, is it?

SEVEN

MORE QUESTIONS ABOUT BUDDHISM ANSWERED

How CAN I BE MORE SPIRITUAL?

*G*ENERALLY, *BEING SPIRITUAL* evokes the idea of a serene person who spends most of their time with joined hands and upturned eyes, maybe singing hymns or chanting, kneeling or sitting on a meditation cushion. This person exists quite apart from the distractions, duties and cares of everyday life. Maybe he or she is a hermit or monastic. Then there is the person's *practice*, which is something different—the doing of something practical.

Here I take *being spiritual* to mean being innately and unconditionally good, and being able to *practice* putting that goodness to use without consciously having to direct your mind along that path. During the spiritual practice I am referring to, the spiritual person is fully aware at all times that there is not one sentient being in existence which doesn't experience suffering. We are all subject to suffering. Any intelligent person who comes to understand that life or existence is constant change knows this. A spiritual person empathizes with others—not abstractly but naturally.

I believe spirituality is what is meant by loving kindness, universal compassion and love for fellow sentient beings who may be in need of what we can give. This kind of spiritual practice isn't necessarily part of religion at all. When I read the works of famous mystics, it seems to me that they often had no choice but to cloak their meaning in the language of religion in order to be understood by their contemporaries, and to avoid torture and death at the hands of fanatics.

There are writings from all the religions that show that a person can belong to any religion, or none at all, and still be a spiritual practitioner. A religion may point the way, but the practitioner treads the path alone simply because that is the sort of person they are or have become.

Anyone can be a spiritual practitioner—You don't have to be a Buddhist or wear robes—but you do need to be aware of suffering and the causes of suffering in every action you carry out.

How Do I Begin on the Path to Enlightenment?

THE PURPOSE OF Buddhist practice is to become enlightened. This is the ultimate goal of any practicing Buddhist. It is easy enough to learn by heart the things to do and not to do—be compassionate, follow the Eightfold Path and so on. But what is this enlightenment we seek?

Enlightenment is seeing existence clearly, as clearly as we possibly can.

There are many types of people who seek enlightenment and want guidance. The old story about three pots applies here. The first pot has a hole in it so that everything that goes in it leaks out. The second pot is so full that nothing else can fit in. The third pot holds what is offered and the contents can be investigated at any time. Some people are like the first pot and grope around in the dark. Others bring all their misconceptions, strongly held opinions, preconceptions and past baggage with them and struggle because of these. And some seem already on the path to enlightenment and are able to learn.

No one, not even the Buddha himself, can *give* us enlightenment. As all the sages tell us, enlightenment is a very personal experience.

Unless we free ourselves of self-deception, we won't get very far at all. This proves difficult because of all sentient beings, we humans are masters at lying to ourselves. We tell ourselves we are never to blame. We don't even play a part in the problems that confront us. We have always tried to do the right thing. Other people and circumstances cause us to deviate from compassion for all suffering sentient beings. Our motives have always—but always—been as pure as the driven snow. With these delusions grasped tightly in our minds we hope to learn to see everything *else* in the clarity of enlightenment.

To make progress on the path to enlightenment, we need to understand ourselves first of all. If we don't look after ourselves, we won't be able to look after anyone else. If we don't understand ourselves, we will never truly understand anything.

The solution to our problems lies in the problem itself—*if* we can bring ourselves to see the problem in all its aspects. As soon as we see the problem clearly, we have the answer, but seeing clearly requires painful honesty on our part. This is where frequent meditation is required. Meditation is the remedy.

Present your problem to your mind, and in quiet meditation allow your thoughts to rise like bubbles in champagne. Don't follow them emotionally one way or the other. Leave the mind's functioning alone. Then with pure motive, use the solution that comes to you, as long as it doesn't harm you or others. When you can do this, you will have at least one sure foot on the path. Remember, nothing worthwhile is gained without effort and honesty toward yourself.

How Are People Converted to Buddhism?

THERE ARE SEVERAL methods in use by persons or organizations to change the opinions of others to their own. I say "opinions," because that is all the converter's ideas are. The following methods head the list: persuasion and bribery, threat and force, and the Buddhist way of *non-conversion*, which is to teach when requested, to set an example by one's own behavior, and never to use coercion.

The first method—persuasion and bribery—has been extensively used by a stronger culture (often backed by ruling authority or superior arms) over another culture. Bribery is in the form of goods and services considered to be superior to those of the indigenous population. This method helps to undermine any beliefs of the weaker culture that conflict with those of the converters. And it incorporates, with appropriate changes by the converters, those beliefs held most dear by those being converted.

When this method is used by religious groups, the converters often act with apparent authority from unshakeable belief in their own opinions. It's obvious that the gods have smiled on the converters in material and technological terms, so their gods must be stronger than the gods of the converted.

The second method—threat and force—is as popular today as it ever has been. In this situation, the people being invaded or converted are labeled with derogatory terms. For the invader or converter it is much easier to destroy a group or race of people to whom you've given a denigrating label than to destroy a sentient being who sometimes, especially if you make eye contact, looks just like your brother, sister, father, mother or child.

The third method—non-conversion—is different. No one can be *converted* to Buddhism. In some cases, you might be converted to Buddhist ways of behavior by the example of Buddhist practitioners. However, real Buddhism is not someone else's opinion. It is a simple and subtle philosophy that must be understood and meditated on before one can be said to be a Buddhist. No bribery, force or persuasion can *make* a person understand a philosophy or *make* a person meditate. These are activities of the individual mind.

Buddhism is spread by request—the rule being to teach when requested, and that's it. In other words, seekers find the teacher and in doing so find themselves. Having chosen the teacher—and this must be carefully done—you must guard against clinging to a teacher as if to a life raft, or fostering a cult of the individual.

There are many excellent teachers, some coming from a slightly different perspective than others. At a certain stage, it is good to listen to different interpretations of Buddhism, provided you don't just jump from opinion to opinion, but *meditate* and come to a conclusion that makes sense to your questing mind.

Remember this: If you are not already seeking, you cannot be converted; and if you are seeking, the process of conversion has already begun. It is personal experience.

WHAT DOES TAKING REFUGE MEAN?

PEOPLE WHO FORMALLY turn to Buddhism formally *"take refuge"* in the Buddha, the Dharma he taught, and the *Sangha* or "community" of enlightened practitioners. They formally vow to keep *the Five Precepts.* Completing this ritual brings them into the community of practicing Buddhists (*Sangha*).

In *taking refuge,* we aren't handing over responsibility for our lives to some deity that can now be seen as the cause of everything that happens to us. What we have really done is accept responsibility for our own actions of body, speech and mind. We have accepted that events involving us don't occur without our having some part in causing them to happen.

In taking refuge, we embark on a never-ending journey of discovery. The success of our journey depends on two things now. First, it depends on our own self-honesty. If we can't be 100 percent honest with ourselves, we're wasting our time. Being completely honest with ourselves is like peeling layers from an onion. Many of the layers will bring out tears of regret, humiliation and pity for what we have done. This isn't judging anyone, not even ourselves. It is simply a clearing out. Until we can be completely honest with ourselves, the path leads nowhere. Blank. No progress. Stalemate.

This is where we need guidance, someone who knows the way, someone we can trust—a teacher. This teacher can be male or female, monastic or a lay practitioner. What makes this person a *teacher* is that he or she knows about the rocks in the path we are on. These are similar for all of us. And he or she uses the Buddha's teachings to show us a smoother way. Later, when we can go ahead on our own, we can extend a helping hand to others setting out.

Taking refuge is the foundation for peace of mind. Buddhists take refuge in the Buddha as enlightenment (the goal), in the Dharma as the teachings, and in the *Sangha* as the enlightened teachers. Then we go forward at our own pace, not trying to run before we learn to walk. Finally, we reach the goal we have set ourselves—whatever that may be.

WHAT IS ZEN?

THE WORD *ZEN* comes from the Sanskrit word *dhyana*, passing through the Chinese word *Chan*, to Japanese *Zen*. It simply means "meditation."

A short extract paraphrased from the teachings of Hui Neng, the Fifth Chan Patriarch of China, will best illustrate the method of *Chan* or *Zen*. Hui Neng (638–713 A.D.), who later became the Sixth Buddhist Patriarch of China, was the son of a Buddhist government official who had been dismissed from his post and died during his son's infancy. As soon as he was old enough, Hui Neng worked hard to support his mother and himself. He became a wood seller, receiving education at his mother's knee and wherever else he could. History tells us he was semi-literate, which is debatable.

One day, after delivering some wood, Hui Neng heard a man in the street reciting a teaching of the Buddha. It was the *Diamond Sutra*—one of the main Buddhist texts. He immediately grasped its meaning and was enlightened. (If one has studied this teaching well and puzzled over it for years, understanding its message most certainly *can* come instantaneously.)

Hui Neng, though allegedly semi-literate, had always been a deep thinker. He soon had the good fortune to be given a gift of money by someone who recognized his worth, and he was advised to go to the monastery of the Fifth Patriarch. He gave his mother the money and went to the monastery in hopes of further education in the Dharma. The Patriarch saw immediately that Hui Neng was already enlightened, but he showed him no favor in order to shield him from jealousy—especially from the head monk, Shen Hsiu, who expected that *he* would be chosen as the next Patriarch.

In order to examine the true state of wisdom of Shen Hsiu as a candidate, the Fifth Patriarch asked all the monks to write a stanza on their understanding of the essence of mind. The Patriarch knew that only Shen Hsiu would attempt this challenge, because the other monks were afraid to compete with someone they considered so much more learned than themselves. Afraid to offer his stanza directly to the Patriarch, Shen Hsiu crept out at night with a lamp and wrote the following stanza on the wall of the south corridor where the Patriarch would be sure to see it next morning:

Our body is the Bodhi tree
And our mind a mirror bright.
Carefully we wipe them, hour by hour
And let no dust alight.

Sutra of Hui Neng (tr. Wong Moulam)

On reading this, the Patriarch knew for sure that Shen Hsiu was not yet enlightened, but he praised the stanza and left it there to help those at or below Shen Hsiu's level of understanding.

Hui Neng heard about the stanza, even though he had spent most of his eight months at the monastery pounding rice in the kitchen. He asked a boy to show it to him, as he had never been in that section of the building. A visiting official was present at that time, and at Hui Neng's request this official read the poem to him. Hui Neng surprised those present by saying that *he* had a stanza, and *he* would like someone to write it for him, which the visitor did. This was the stanza:

There is no Bodhi tree
Nor stand of a mirror bright
Since all is void {empty of inherent existence}
Where can the dust alight?

Sutra of Hui Neng (tr. Wong Moulam)

There is of course much more to share from the autobiography of Hui Neng, but the difference in understanding between these two stanzas shows how *Zen* gets immediately to the point of the foundation of Buddhist philosophy.

Zen stories make delightful reading for some people, but they can seem infuriatingly obscure to others. I still recall my own reaction to the first piece of Zen literature I ever read—infuriation! "Why the hell can't they just say what they mean?" I fumed. Then I studied and puzzled and meditated until I was thoroughly fed up and put it aside for quite some time. It was not until much later that the penny dropped, as the saying goes.

My inability to understand was due in part to my own unimaginative mind—too rational and pedantic—and in part to my lack of a proper teacher. I had jumped in without having learned to swim or even to dog-paddle. I had wanted to see everything from a very practical point of view. Quite suddenly I realized there was nothing to see. There was no such thing as a bodhi tree, no such thing as a mirror bright or otherwise. All conditioned phenomena are, by definition, without inherent existence.

This is *zen*.

What Is a Retreat, and What Can It Do for Me?

A RETREAT IS not simply a pleasant, relaxing holiday in serene surroundings with a dash of spiritual guidance thrown in. A true retreat will be the hardest mental activity we have ever undertaken if we are seeking to change our outlook. No soothing music, no repeated affirmation of our individual worth by a facilitator, no swapping of stories in a cozy group therapy session.

Not all retreats are the same, of course. There are many different types of retreats based on different types of motivation. The type I describe is like a *mind cleansing* in preparation for understanding Buddhist philosophy. The purpose of this type of retreat is to learn insight—insight, first of all, into our own mind. For this purpose we need to be mentally and physically still, undisturbed by everyday concerns. No phone calls, no mail, no visitors, no radio, television or music.

Usually, our days are filled with mental and physical activity. Much of this is necessary for our survival and well-being and for the survival and well-being of those dependent on us. Yet if we are honest with ourselves, a good deal of this activity is unnecessary. We use it to fill in those spaces we fear when nothing seems to be happening, or to prevent something we don't want to happen from happening.

In order to gain insight in retreat, we have to come face to face with what we do and why we do it. We have to seek out our motives without shame or blame in an effort to see things clearly. This is why silence is the next most important requirement after freedom from everyday concerns. Silence is essential, no matter what is going on, because we must, as quickly as possible, be able to turn our attention to ourselves. This may sound egotistical, but it is easy when one is in close contact with strangers for a certain length of time to become irritated by the actions of others. We need to keep reminding ourselves that what the others are doing is not our business. And there's not much point discussing our problems with other retreatants at this stage for they are, like us, stumbling along trying to sort out their own difficulties.

The only break in silence during a retreat might be for the purpose of interviews with a spiritual guide or retreat facilitator.

You may consider interviews with a spiritual guide—if there is one—to be unnecessary. You may feel confident about solving your own problems. There may be things you don't want to expose to another person, however impartial that person may be. Nevertheless, it is often extremely beneficial to verbalize a problem in order to solve it. Just finding the words to express it as concisely as possible often triggers a mental solution. The spiritual guide isn't there to judge, but only to be a sounding board and to offer practical advice on a different way of viewing the problem or handling it. You will be the one to find the solution. That is the only way introspection can become insight.

You will know you've had a good retreat if at first you become irritated, even really angry, then decide to leave the next day, then hate all the other retreatants and the food, then go almost crazy with sheer boredom and then, at last, see the light at the end of the tunnel!

This type of strict retreat may sound like torture but it is, in fact, wonderfully mind cleansing. It is a necessary basis for further understanding oneself and the Buddhist path. We usually fail to realize how cluttered our minds actually are with what Buddhists like to describe as "drunken monkey chatter." Our mental chatter needs to be quieted down before we can learn anything.

This kind of short, strict retreat isn't oriented in any particular direction. It is more like getting to know oneself.

It does not always work to do this in familiar settings. We can't just close the front door and take the phone off the hook. Callers will interrupt our retreat. The household pet will need attention and food. The mail will arrive and a great deal of will power will be needed to ignore it. Children will arrive home from school hungry or in tears, and then our partner will arrive home. It seems fairly hopeless, doesn't it? Well, it is—until we learn how to retreat at any time and place, until meditation becomes a constant state of mind.

We don't necessarily need to become a hermit, but we do need a few things. The first thing we need is a suitable place for retreat. The second is some sort of a guide, not so much an instructor but a guide.

Again, the place of retreat needs to be as quiet as possible, away from traffic, crowds and the distractions of everyday life. You may own such a space—a beach house, a hideaway. Ideally, there should be food available with little effort on your part, and reasonable, even makeshift, facilities for cleanliness. Don't bother searching too hard and too long for the right place. When you are ready the place will in some way be presented to you. Be prepared to take the leap into what is, as yet, unknown. The peace of the retreat will seep into you if you persevere and fully absorb it.

Next, the guide. Those who want to discover more about the Buddha's teachings can often manage well with certain books and tapes. But the beginner often needs a guide. The best help comes from a guide who is simply there for you, someone you consider to know more than you do, who hears what you say with strict confidentiality and an absence of judgment. The duty of the guide is simply to assist in preparing the beginning retreatant to be *able* to retreat.

If you are one of those people who has been dabbling in these subjects and promising yourself to go into retreat (some do this for years on end), why not pick up the phone, send an E-mail and book yourself into a retreat center? You won't regret it.

Go on. I dare you.

ℋow Did You Become a Buddhist Nun?

INCENSE WAS FIRMLY molded with wax into small cones, three of which were placed in line across the freshly shaven scalp of each of six women dressed in gray sitting cross-legged on the floor. A burning taper was then applied to each cone in turn. As the cones smoldered, tears slid from under the lowered eyelids of one of the women, while some of the others pressed their lips together firmly. The onlookers, also dressed in gray, almost held their breath watching for signs of weakness, perhaps even hoping for them. On one head, a cone crumbled and fell in tiny burning fragments onto the garments of the woman. She made no move. A fresh cone was molded, reapplied to her head, and lit. Because the woman involved in this mishap was the oldest in the group, she was watched carefully and compassionately by those in charge of the ordeal.

After fifteen or twenty minutes, the cones had completely burned up, and antiseptic dressings were applied to the women's burned scalps. The six women then rose and bowed deeply toward the officiants and to the onlookers who had quietly encouraged them. The sufferers now donned yellow robes over their gray ones, and the number of patches making up each yellow robe indicated that these women were Buddhist nuns.

What had been going on here? Who were these women? Who were the people in charge? Who was being tested? By whom? And to what purpose?

The women dressed only in gray were Vietnamese laywomen. The ones undergoing the burning were ordained Buddhist nuns who had the previous day received the highest ordination. The nationalities of the six nuns were Australian, Dutch, French, Spanish and Vietnamese. I was the one on whose scalp the cone had crumbled.

The ceremony, which we had just been part of, was undertaken voluntarily, both from respect for custom and from personal conviction. It was also the last part of a three-day ritual, and the public part of our ordination ceremonies—this part was the taking of *bodhisattva* vows, a solemn Mahayana Buddhist initiation. We initiates vowed to direct all our efforts toward helping every sentient being attain enlightenment. Now by silently enduring the burning we were "putting our money where the mouth is," so to speak, and proving our commitment to suffer whatever might be necessary to fulfill our vows.

Does it hurt? It certainly does. As to who is testing whom, the answer is that we were each testing ourselves because of an inner need to do so. The people in charge were the senior monks and nuns involved in the ordination ceremonies the previous day. It was done entirely in a spirit of love and support, with no pressure applied at any point by anyone.

Not all present-day sects of Buddhist religion practice this ritual. Today more than five years after my full ordination (I was a novice for twelve years), my hair is long and I wear it in a bun. My scars could be noticed only by a hairdresser, if I ever used one, when I am residing in a monastery. They are of no interest to anyone but myself. Some monks and nuns go through this burning ceremony more than once, adding new scars to old. Why they do this only they know for sure. I can only speak for myself—I made a commitment that doesn't need reviving. I did so in a Vietnamese temple, near Limoges, France.

I am often asked why—not how—I, a Western woman of some worldly experience, was initially attracted to the teachings of the Buddha. Here is the best explanation I can give, although, like all humans beings, I am no expert at seeing my own motives and reasons with fullest clarity.

My interest in ancient history, anthropology, archaeology, mythology, religion and mysticism (all nurtured by the books my father used to send me once I turned fourteen) resulted in a lack of satisfaction with the didactic tenets of the main religions—Hinduism, Judaism, Christianity and Islam. I am the type of person who dislikes being told what to do unless I understand, at least to some extent, what the expected result might be.

I was a very religious child, educated partly in Catholic schools, and I regularly attended rituals of my religion. I wanted very much to *believe* as others seemed able to do, to have a sure faith with no nagging questions being asked by my questioning mind. Consequently, I tried to find satisfactory answers in many Christian sects. Although I met many sincere, kind people in my journey, those who professed to be teachers were of no help where my questions were concerned.

I read the Old and New Testaments many times. In view of my early reading of ancient history and mythology the Old Testament seemed patently to be tribal interpretation of earlier history from other cultures. This undermined my ability to take its offshoot, Christianity, on faith alone. At the same time I envied, and still do, those who have strong faith and ability to believe what they don't understand. This peace of mind was not for me. I didn't realize then that what I was seeking was not so much a religion but a philosophy to live by which would make sense of existence.

I found present-day Islam's ideas of paradise as instant reward for death in a holy war—and also the Muslim attitude toward women—distasteful, although I admired the actual social teachings of the prophet Mohammed and found much of Sufism appealing. I found Hinduism fascinating as a historical and philosophical study, but not as a religion for me.

I was looking for answers that made sense of the general muddle that life seemed to me to be. Nowhere, except in the early teachings of the Buddha, did I find a way to discover those answers.

It is not my intention to denigrate the beliefs held by others. The impulse to religious belief is an integral part of human nature, which may take many forms. One's final understanding will be a personal experience that cannot be forced on others or even branded as "the truth."

Really, words are not of much use in matters above and beyond language. We are a mentally lazy lot, not aware of how much mind and brain power we have and forever seeking salvation handed to us on a platter. Salvation from what? The only thing I felt we needed salvation from was our own ignorance. This must be a unique personal experience. Others, including the Buddha, can only point the way.

This was what I was seeking. Have I found what I was seeking? Yes. Am I able to put it to proper use? I am practicing to do so, but there is no end to this practicing. Even enlightenment would not be an end, only another beginning.

The most valuable thing I have learned is to take personal responsibility for my actions and reactions as they influence present and future moments. If I mess it up, I don't look for someone or something else to blame. I am always free to choose my next step, and accept the consequences.

To me, this is a wonderful freedom and security—if there is any such thing. It doesn't make me any wiser as a person but it does mean that there is no one I have finally to answer to but myself. And I practice living so that this answering may be as easy as possible.

It is my sincere hope that all beings will eventually find all the questions and answers each one of us seeks to find.

(On Which It Is Hoped No One Will Wholly Agree with the Answers)

IT'S GOOD TO question, especially in matters of religion where one is often expected to accept what is imparted purely on faith. Questioning is not the same as doubting. To question is to seek further information. Questioning is not always a sign of not knowing. Often it is simply a desire for clarification if the source of information seems obscure. Yet in religion, the questioner is often made to feel guilty of a crime not only against the instructor but against the very deity itself.

The competent Buddhist teacher respects those who question as serious seekers-after-wisdom or knowledge. Questions are indications of the seeker's level of understanding and philosophical outlook on life.

To question is to learn, even if the answers are not necessarily always correct—provided the questioner goes on to question the answers.

It is not always comfortable to be a questioner living in a community of believers who may judge the "unbeliever" to be blasphemous, but questioning is well worth it in the long run. This is my personal reason for spending more time in the lay community than in large communities of monks and nuns.

Finally, I'd like to answer questions most commonly asked of me by non-Buddhists regarding what they may have read, observed or been told of Buddhist practices and doctrines. At the same time, I hope you won't believe the answers. I hope you will insist on investigating until you can experience for yourself the truth or otherwise of what I say.

Q: *Why did the Buddha bother to teach when there was already in place at least one religion with all the authority of an upper class in charge of it?*

A: From the teachings it becomes apparent that the Brahmin and Jain religions in Indian during the sixth century B.C. had become extremely ritualized. The Brahmin religion was filled with superstition and based largely on animal sacrifice, without the animal itself being considered in any way sacred. The important part of the Brahmin sacrifice was blood. The poor, who were most in need of blessings, became even poorer as they attempted to gain blessings by giving the Brahmin priests animals and birds to offer to the myriad deities. The deeper philosophy behind the origins of this religion was being lost.

At this time, there were many like the Buddha who, once family duty was done, left the comforts of domesticity and wandered about seeking to understand why there was so much ignorance, greed, lack of lasting satisfaction and suffering in life. It was a time when some people believed physical deprivation and painful suffering would free the mind for greater understanding. Some believed in overindulgence. Others worshipped fire and even ingested only water and one particular type of herb or weed. These practices often produced deep trances, which were regarded as great attainments, and hallucinations brought about by starvation, which were considered revelations.

For seven years, Siddhartha Gautama tried all the methods recommended by acknowledged sages and found no satisfactory answers in them. There had to be another way.

The motivation for the Buddha's quest was compassion—compassion for suffering sentient beings, not only for himself. He didn't set out to found a religion or establish monasteries. These were merely natural progressions as more and more people came to follow him and to attempt to grasp what he taught. He did not set out to undermine the prevailing religions, but when someone came to discuss their beliefs with him he did his best to stimulate the speaker to deeper thought.

The Buddha taught for more than half his life, but it won't necessarily take that long for a persevering seeker to learn what he taught. For us it is questioning, not faith, that is needed for proper comprehension of the teachings of Buddha Sakyamuni, Sage of the World.

Q: *Are there Buddhist teachings regarding heaven and hell?*
A: No, there are not. The teachings are metaphors for states of mind experienced in this life.

Q: *Is the Dalai Lama the Buddhist 'Pope'?*
A: No. His Holiness the Dalai Lama is, as he often states, a simple Tibetan Buddhist monk, head of the Gelugpa sect. The special reverence paid to him by Tibetans is due to their belief in his being the reincarnation of the Buddha of compassion. This is a Tibetan Buddhist concept stemming from anthropomorphizing an abstract idea of the compassionate potential in all beings.

Q: *Is the Mahayana school more "Buddhist" than the Theravada?*
A: No. The basic tenets of both are Buddhist. Each differs on

some philosophical points that developed after the Buddha's death.

Q: *Why must nuns take so many more vows than monks?*

A: The greater number of vows for nuns is often seen as anti-women. Although it wouldn't be correct for me to go into detail on this point (unless to a woman seeking ordination), it is a fact that many of the extra vows were for the protection of nuns when they were not living in monasteries. Delightful as it would be if women (and men) could travel in safety at all times and not have their appearance or demeanor misinterpreted, this was not, and is not, the case *anywhere.* Buddhism deals with facts, not what ought to be. Although many of the vows have been made irrelevant by time, they have been preserved in the monastic rules, and the right-minded nun acts accordingly.

Q: *Do women have the opportunity to become leaders?*

A: Definitely, if that is their way. They may become teachers or heads of monasteries. They are often revered by their followers and disciples.

Q: *Are monks considered to be "higher" than nuns?*

A: In a monastery this may appear to be so, but this is a matter for individuals. A learned monk or nun is respected, gender notwithstanding. Attitudes based on gender are cultural, not Buddhist.

Q: *Is it considered that only monastics may become enlightened?*

A: Definitely not. There are no such beliefs in Buddhism. There have been, and one hopes there will continue to be, many dedicated lay teachers demonstrating high attainments. Some have been monks or nuns. Some have never contemplated the monastic life.

Q: *Why would someone brought up as a Christian, Jew, Hindu, Muslim or in any other religion, turn to Buddhism for answers?*

A: Obviously, for the serious seeker-after-wisdom or knowledge, the answer is that the religion in which they were raised has failed to give satisfactory answers. The cause of this lack of lasting satisfaction is often the fault of those who see themselves as knowledgeable teachers but who don't fully understand the tenets of their own religion, and who discourage questions they cannot answer. For the intelligent questing mind, this often leads to confusion and outright disbelief, and may stunt the desire for investigation. Hearing and reading something of Buddhist philosophy, the seeker may decide to go on with the search.

The variety of people attracted to Buddhism from other religions is as diverse as there are human psychological characteristics, some being attracted more to the culture than to the religion.

Q: *Why do Buddhist monks and nuns shave their heads?*

A: In the days of the Buddha, as today, hair was a person's crowning glory. People spent much time caring for it and dressing it with jewels and flowers for personal satisfaction and for attracting attention. As the *Sangha* grew, this was found not to be in the interests of serious study. Therefore, it became the custom that on ordination one's "crowning glory" was shorn—a sign of renunciation of both vanity and the desire for admiration.

When one lives under monastic conditions, a shaven head arouses no interest, but if one lives outside the monastery, it's best to do what is most appropriate in the circumstances. Being the only Buddhist I know of in the country town where I live, to be jeered at by some young people as a "skinhead" (in my seventies!) would seem to be calling down ridicule on this practice and perhaps, therefore, on Buddhism in the minds of those with little or no knowledge of it. Therefore, I do not shave my head.

Q: *What is the Buddhist attitude to marriage?*

A: Much the same as in Christianity, Judaism or Islam, marriage is seen as a contract between a man and a woman to love, honor and cherish each other and the children of their union.

Adultery is contrary to the Buddhist precept of no unlawful sexual activity. Divorce is a civil, not a religious, matter.

Q: *Isn't Buddhism a sexist, patriarchal religion?*

A: No. To a practicing Buddhist, especially a religious one believing in reincarnation, men and women change places often in other lives so that one sees people just as people, no matter what sex they may be in this life. The philosophic Buddhist knows that, male or female, we are *all* suffering sentient beings—right now.

Q: *Don't Buddhists pray to be reborn as males so they can achieve enlightenment?*

A: No. This idea is very much pre-Buddhist and a hangover in some cultures—popular with those whom it flatters.

Q: *Must all Buddhist monks and nuns always wear their robes?*

A: Not when it is inappropriate. For those who live and work in a Western-style society where there is no lay financial support, whatever is appropriate may be worn. However, one's robes are always carried even when traveling in lay clothes. This is symbolized by carrying special scraps of yellow cloth. A monk or nun has vowed not to be without one's robes, begging bowl or water strainer. These are constant reminders of one's ordination vows.

Q: *How can one know which is the most suitable sect to approach?*

A: My advice is to study as much as you can of all of them. On the other hand, it doesn't really matter where you begin, because you will soon find *your* way if you continually investigate what you are told. My first interest was in the Southern School teachings (*Theravada*), but the nearest place of instruction was Tibetan (*Mahayana*) so I began there. Now many years later I call myself simply a "Buddha Buddhist," and I am deeply thankful to *all* who have helped me find my way along the path.

Q: *Is it a fact that Buddhists shouldn't be interested in increasing their possessions?*

A: No. At no time has Buddhism ever advocated voluntary poverty. Buddhism does teach what all people know—that wealth doesn't insulate us from suffering and that to exploit other sentient beings for gain is unethical. In fact, the Buddha in fact advised wealthy people and business people on how to remain prosperous and to pay a fair day's pay for a fair day's work!

EIGHT

A FINAL WORD

$\mathcal{D}$OES MY TALK of no thing, no self, no soul and the interconnection of all that exists—the dependent-arising of whatever exists at any given nanosecond (or less)—leave you feeling alone, adrift, transparent and of no importance? Think again.

What the concepts of no thing, no self, no soul and dependent-arising don't highlight is that *each part of the whole is unique.* It follows that you too are unique. In the entire world there is not one other you. Many may share similarities, physical and mental, but the complete package is one of a kind. It also follows that you are not invisible—you are outstanding. You are a powerhouse of positive energy generated by what we label "the self."

That energy needs to be channeled toward some goal or it will simply dissipate. Only you can direct it.

Don't fritter it away until old age naturally reduces it and leaves you sighing "if only." Don't let yourself become depressed because someone hurts or makes fun of you. Ask yourself who and what that person really is and why they act this way. Tell yourself the truth about your true ability and potential. You can do anything with your own potential. If you develop your powers of observation and concentration, you can achieve your goal, whatever it may be. As a Buddhist, I hope your goal will be enlightenment!

Buddhist training will help you fulfill your potential. This training isn't just to help you meditate and develop loving kindness and compassion for sentient beings. It enables you to be the best you can be. Do you want power? Then the Dharma will give you power—power over your own mind, power to control that mind and set it on the best path. The Buddha said that where the mind goes, there the body goes. Surely you've seen your attention fasten securely on something until you're drawn in that direction, and finally get there. Like everything the mind does, this can be used to your advantage or otherwise. You can act skillfully or unskillfully depending on the clarity of your awareness and your degree of mind control.

Nothing that you can think of—nothing in the whole of existence—is unchanging, everlasting or eternal. You may think that the change involved in a rose blooming and dying happens faster than the natural wearing away of a block of granite. But even as the bud is opening, the stone is changing. It is all relative.

If you can be aware of constant change, you won't be overcome or defeated by suffering. Your expectations will be based on well thought out probabilities, and if they don't happen, you'll know you did your best. You will have learned a few limits of your assumptions, and you will do better the next time.

This kind of mind control takes as much practice as mastering a sport, a musical instrument or certain machines.

Self-confidence may not come easily to you. When you look ahead, you may see yourself as you are now, lacking self-confidence, seeing yourself as not having achieved anything. But you have forgotten impermanence—you are changing constantly, and everything else is changing, too. The person you will be isn't the person you are at this moment when you fear and doubt the future. Don't view the future with yourself lost and bewildered in it. You are as important a part of the whole of existence as any other. Remember, each one of us contains within ourselves a great potential to be whatever we wish to be.

And don't let my rather cut-and-dried way of discussing the Buddha's teachings take all the color and wonder out of it for you. This is just my way of approach—my personal way. The Dharma is not simply to be accepted as a terrific philosophical theory. It needs to be personally experienced to be fully understood. It took

me years to understand—insofar as I do—the teaching on emptiness, and it took just as long to understand why at that point I
hadn't sprouted a halo of light and a beautific smile, and why I
could still experience annoyance and sadness.

With my pragmatic way of speaking of the Dharma, it may
seem I am denying any spiritual value to be found in Buddhism.
This would be wrong for me to do. There is color, wonder and a
deep mysticism in the Dharma. Mysticism is usually thought of as
exclusive to theistic religions. This isn't so. True mystics are actually beyond religion. They travel farther than the average seeker,
but what they learn can only be translated into the language of religion if it's to be intelligible. Otherwise the mystic is considered a
witch or wizard, becoming the star at the next public bonfire.

How can what can't be thought be explained? Perhaps
through music, allegorical paintings, sculpture, poetry and
prose—obliquely. There are many ways, yet they are still only
signposts. The moon's reflection in water is lovely and inspiring
but the reflection is not the moon. Words, music, paintings,
poetry, chanting, statues, candles and incense only assist our
one-pointed concentration. They are only signposts.

Many of us find it easier to look pious and just lean on the sign-
post. This is our individual choice, to remain at ease or to dare to
journey forward. If we decide to go forward, it is to understand
ourselves and our motives for what we do. Until we have analyzed
the reasons for our own thoughts, words and deeds with scrupu-
lous honesty, we can't really understand anything else. Yet once

this difficult and painful step is taken, the rest becomes easier. It is as though we had cleared something thorny from our path.

Once we have cleared our minds, dropped our guilt and old resentments and stopped trying to be omniscient, it is amazing what can now enter the mind unhindered and seemingly unsought. What enters is not from outside or from other powers. It is the freeing of our own intuition, our own inner wisdom that was always there.

It is my fervent wish that this short discourse on Buddhism might put aside some of the cultural veils that have obscured the Buddha's original teachings. I hope it may encourage tolerance for a religion that isn't a threat to any other.

People can't be forced to believe something. This applies especially to Buddhist philosophy, where belief depends on personal experience. We can talk to someone about a wonderful or horrifying experience and describe it in detail, but the other person will never fully understand or *believe* what they are told without the opportunity to assess the matter fully for themselves. We can't know exactly what another person is feeling, even though we may have had very similar experiences. Being in a small boat at sea in a hurricane can be brilliantly described, losing a loved one to illness can be discussed, the safe birth of a child can be talked about—but no one can know what any of these experiences is like until they *experience* the same or a very similar condition. True understanding and *real* belief can come only from personal *experience*. Buddhism is a *personal* experience. I hope to have made this very clear.

Finally, I wouldn't be a true Buddhist if I didn't hope that some of my readers will want to know more. You don't need to look in hidden, far-off places for wisdom. All that's needed is the sincere desire to learn, then the way will be opened. Any Buddhist center with a library has material for you to begin your investigations and understanding of the Dharma.

I haven't gone beyond a certain point in explaining Buddhist practice because I have neither the wish nor the ability. The Buddhist teachings are graduated teachings. They require personal contact between a teacher and student to be of real use. This takes deep commitment on both sides and time for the teacher to explore and comprehend the student's understanding.

Buddhism can be taught on many levels. With continuing study and practice it will become like a never-empty treasure chest for you. You will think you have extracted everything in a certain teaching, yet when you come back to it you find even greater treasures. This is because you are persevering in expanding your own understanding and personal experience.

My last word to you is the Buddha's message—"Be a light to yourselves." This book will have done what it was meant to do if you don't believe a word of it without thoroughly investigating what is written.

Does it make sense to you? Does it stimulate you mentally to figure it out for yourself?

It doesn't matter if you aren't following the Buddhist teachings *exactly* the same as another person does, or indeed as the

Buddha did. Seek your own enlightenment with diligence, with the Buddhist teachings in mind.

May your journey be blessed.

$\mathcal{A}$s THIS BOOK is not written in order to teach anyone Buddhist philosophy, merely to whet the appetite of those so interested, there is no particular work recommended as a beginning. It really does not matter where one begins because, if the interest is there, one choice will lead to others.

Bahm, A. J. *Philosophy of the Buddha*. Fremont, Calif.: Jain Publishing Co., 1958.

Batchelor, Stephen. *The Faith to Doubt*. Berkeley: Parrallax Press, 1990.

The Book of Kindred Sayings, trans. F. L. Woodward. Boston: Wisdom Publications, 1980.

Buddhist Studies Review. Copies obtainable from R. Webb, 31 Russell Chambers, Bury Place, London WC1A 2JK.

The Dalai Lama [Tenzin Gyatso]. *Freedom in Exile*. San Francisco: HarperSanFrancisco, 2000.

The Dalai Lama [Tenzin Gyatso]. *The Good Heart*, trans. Thupten Jinpa, ed. Robert Kiely. Boston: Wisdom Publications, 1998.

The Diamond Sutra and the Sutra of Hui Neng, trans. A. F. Price and Wong Mou-Lam, Boston: Shambhala Publications, 1990.

Guenther, Herbert V. and Chogyam Trungpa. *The Dawn of Tantra*. Boston: Shambhala Publications, 2001.

Huyen-Vi, Thich *The Life and Works of Sariputta Thera*, 2nd edition, Paris: Linh-Son Research Institute, 1989.

Kalapahana, David J. *A History of Buddhist Philosophy*. Honolulu: University of Hawaii Press, 1992.

Keown, Damien. *The Nature of Buddhist Ethics*. New York: Palgrave Macmillan, 1992.

Ling, Trevor. *The Buddha*. Aldershot, England: Gower Publishing Ltd., 1973.

The Long Discourses of the Buddha, trans. Maurice Walsh. Boston: Wisdom Publications, 1987.

Mizuno, Kogen. *The Beginnings of Buddhism*, trans. Richard L. Gage. Tokyo: Kosei Publishing Co., 1992.

Pande, G. C. *Studies in the Origins of Buddhism*. 5th ed. Delhi: Molilal Banarsides, 1974.

Payutto, P. A. *Good, Evil and Beyond*, trans. Bruce Evans. Bankok: Buddhadhamma Foundation, 1996.

Rahula, Walpola. *What the Buddha Taught*. New York: Grove Press, 1986.

Rinpoche, Sogyal. *The Tibetan Book of Living and Dying*. San Francisco: HarperSanFrancisco, 2002.

The Tibetan Book of the Dead, trans. W. Y. Evans-Wentz, Kathmandu: Pilgrims Publishing, 1998.

Trungpa, Chogyam. *Born in Tibet*. 4th ed. Boston: Shambhala Publications, 2000.

[ACKNOWLEDGMENTS]

𝒥 CAN'T THANK by name the many scholars and philosophers whose works have contributed to my knowledge of Buddhism, nor all the kind teachers who have personally spoken with me. This book is a distillation of my understanding of what they sought to teach, filtered through my own experience and—where mistakes occur—my own lack of understanding.

My gratitude goes out to all my teachers, lay and monastic, male and female, Tibetan, Vietnamese and Western. My sincere thanks go to those Buddhist practitioners who remained my friends despite my seemingly unorthodox views and my tendency to find something amusing in what, to many, may be unquestioned sacred truths. I am also grateful to my friends for their patience in listening to me as I searched for the clearest way to convey what I wanted to say.

I thank my sons for accepting me as I am and for the title of this book. When it was first suggested to me, I laughed. But very soon I realized that *The Naked Buddha* was exactly what I was trying to describe.

And especially I thank my cousin Norma, her daughter Andrea, Deb, May Cuanne and Mary Wood for their help, and my publishers and editors for their belief in my efforts.

APR 13